DEC 2 0 2021

Sticks 'n Stones:
The Myers Family in Levittown
Second Edition

DAISY D. MYERS

Red Land Community Library
70 Newberry Commons
Etters, PA 17319

**YORK COUNTY HISTORY CENTER
YORK, PENNSYLVANIA**

This publication has been produced using funds from
The Robert P. Turner Publication Fund

© 2005, 2021 The Myers Family. Reprinted with permission.

ISBN 978-0-578-30449-6

All rights reserved. No part of this work may be reproduced or used in any form or by any means—electronic of mechanical, including photocopying or by digital means—without written permission from the copyright holder.

Printed by Ream Printing Co., Inc.
York, PA

This book may be purchased from:

York County History Center
250 East Market Street
York, Pennsylvania 17403

www.yorkhistorycenter.org

Phone: 717-848-1587

ILLUSTRATION CREDITS. Charlotte Brooks, photographer, *LOOK Magazine* Collection, Library of Congress, Prints & Photographs Division, Washington, DC; *Pittsburgh Post-Gazette* Pittsburgh, Pennsylvania; Schintz Studio, York, Pennsylvania; Temple University Libraries Urban Archives, Philadelphia, Pennsylvania; *York Daily Record,* York, Pennsylvania.

To my husband, Bill, and the children – William, Stephen, Lynda, and Barry

Contents

	Foreword, First Edition George M. Leader	vii
	Foreword, Second Edition Michael Newsome	ix
	Preface and Acknowledgments Daisy D. Myers	xi
	Introduction Daisy D. Myers	xiii
Chapter 1.	Moving Day	1
Chapter 2.	My Early Years	9
Chapter 3.	Above the Mason-Dixon Line	15
Chapter 4.	The Decision Is Made	21
Chapter 5.	The First Week in Levittown	27
Chapter 6.	Living Under Guard	41
Chapter 7.	The Public Eye	47
Chapter 8.	Meetings and More Meetings	57
Chapter 9.	Little Rock Comes to Levittown	65
Chapter 10.	Peace Finally Comes Home	73
Chapter 11.	Our Day in Court	81
Chapter 12.	The Aftermath	87
Chapter 13.	The Myers Family Moves On	99
	Epilogue Lynda P. Myers	103

Foreword, *First Edition*

The benefits of living in a democratic society in America have not come easy to our African American brothers and sisters.

The fight for equal educational opportunities came as they passed through lines of troops.

The right to vote was denied in many settings and tampered with even up to the present time.

The right to equal employment opportunities is still not the rule and is often the exception.

The right to equal housing opportunities, while not denied legally, is still many times honored in the breach.

This story of Daisy Myers and her family tells us just how painful this discrimination in housing could be for one family with two small sons and a baby daughter.

If Daisy Myers had set out to write a novel, it could not have been more dramatic, delivered a stronger message, or struck a heavier blow in favor of honest, decent, and Christian behavior on the part of the white community.

The dark side is that in the twentieth century so many people could be so unenlightened. The bright side is that Pennsylvania and the world had so many idealistic, compassionate people willing to express themselves and even come forward with tangible evidence of their support.

Both Bill and Daisy were educated, Bill from Pennsylvania and Daisy from Virginia. Good education was available, although in both cases the Myerses were exposed to segregation. The twentieth century was a transitional century insofar as segregation was concerned. But the twenty-first century still has much left to accomplish.

It seems to me that change comes, in the main, because of our heroes: Martin Luther King, Ralph Bunche, the Reverend Ralph Abernathy, Rosa Parks, Jackie Robinson, and many others whose names are not widely known.

I think the time has come to add to that list of heroes the names of Bill and Daisy Myers.

The Honorable George M. Leader
Governor of Pennsylvania, 1955–1959

Foreword, *Second Edition*

Look for yourself among the characters in this story. You are there and so are friends of yours. I saw myself there, and some of my acquaintances. All of us, all Americans, are represented in these pages. Each of us can fit neatly in some aspect of this story.

Levittown, Pennsylvania, could easily be Anytown, USA. The fact that it's a Northern city should give us some pause, since the North was reputed to be much more forgiving and racially tolerant than Americans in other areas of the country.

This is a love story. It is also a story of hate and one of friend and foe. It epitomizes ignorance and celebrates acts of courage, on both sides of the street. It challenges the sensibilities and asks questions we must address in our own lives today, while reflecting on the times. These pages are filled with elation and excitement, anticipation and anger. We cannot ignore the pain and despair reflected herein.

Each of us has had a dream fulfilled or deferred. Each of us has been compelled to help a friend in need, and unfortunately, some of us have instigated the need in others, whether we are willing to admit it or not. We all have at some point in our lives sought after or envisioned, and many achieved, the American dream. But on the path to their dream, the Myers family hit speed bumps of hate and racism, prompting Daisy to ask: "What of the American ideal of justice and equality?"

I have personal connections with this family, having met and conversed with its matriarch. I even spoke with Governor George Leader, whose original foreword to this work was so poignant at the time. But more than that: As I ventured through these pages, the connection of Hampton, Virginia, the town where I was born and raised, and Hampton Institute, where I worked while in high school, dredged up reflections of my life in the 1960s, about a decade after this event. York County, Pennsylvania, is my home now, and such a connection in this saga is a stark reminder of raising my children in this Northern town, a return to my younger days at their age, witnessing some of the same types of events decades later. The Myers' story is still being played out today in York County and America, in modern-day terms, differently but with eerily similar results.

The story of the Myers family is all too familiar throughout Black America, representing fear of the unknown and misconception of the known among White America. The antagonists in the story are well-known and all too familiar. This reminds me of a statement from Daisy Myers: "We have always felt that Negroes have too long been expected to ask for permission for what they deserve."

Today, much of the "asking" continues and much of the lack of permission prevails. We have come a long way, but many overt activities of the 1950s and throughout the twentieth century have become more sophisticated and subtle today. Redlining, while overt last century, has morphed into disparate real estate appraisals for black homeowners this century, less overt but just as harmful. The overt acts of racism and hate experienced by Daisy and her family are reflected less directly in the failure to invoke real housing policy and neighborhood reform, which are manifested in an inferior education system, particularly in the inner cities.

I enjoyed my times with the late Governor Leader, the first governor from York County. I have a much closer connection to the second governor from York County, Tom Wolf. Having worked in his family business and currently serving as his secretary of administration, I have had the honor to witness firsthand the policies his administration has put into place to improve the lives of people of color. That comes in procurement, business loans, education, and so many other areas – and I've witnessed his rebuffed attempts to improve school funding for education and property tax reform to benefit all Pennsylvanians. These two governors from York County have championed the civil rights of all citizens and excoriated such acts experienced and detailed in this recounting.

Bill and Daisy Myers didn't set out to be heroes or to break any new ground. They just wanted a good home for their family, a home that met their criteria of comfort. They did not achieve early comfort. They were met with "stick 'n stones." Law and order was needed, and eventually they received what they deserved, thanks, in part, to Governor Leader's intervention. Peace finally came, but they paid a handsome price. Daisy Myers observed, "Law and order must prevail, but law and order can also maintain the status quo, and that's precisely what Negroes are determined to change."

Please read these pages with an inquisitive and open mind. Ask your own set of questions about the America you know and the America the Myers family experienced. Is that the America we all should know, the America we all deserve?

This experiment of a nation has prevailed despite its shortcomings. Hope and victory can be achieved along the way. Should it be this hard to achieve the goal? Finally, ask how you can personally make it easier for all citizens of this nation to feel at home, wherever they live. At the very least, every American family deserves that.

Michael Newsome is Secretary of Governor Tom Wolf's Office of Administration.

Preface and Acknowledgments

I started writing the text for what would become this book in August 1957, before I knew how the narrative would turn out. I was trying to keep a log of what was happening, more or less for our children because they were so young. Emmett Till's murder had happened only two years before our move to Levittown. The civil rights struggle had started, and I felt we were part of the history.

Support came from all over. I had met the writer Pearl S. Buck through a mutual friend, and she encouraged me to write everything down while it was still fresh. "I've been in your situation," she said, because they were the only white family among the Chinese population, "and I know what it is to be discriminated against." She read the manuscript, provided suggestions, and offered to write a foreword for me. I'll never forget her.

Many, many people have helped me with the writing and the publication of this book. I'm afraid I'm not going to remember some of the names, but I don't want to forget anybody. So many people helped us. Some came from New York, from Philadelphia, just offering whatever assistance they could give, whatever they could do to help us. I can't say enough good about the people who stayed by us. Without them we couldn't have made it.

I want to thank Governor George M. Leader for his support and encouragement at the time and his contribution to the book. I also want to thank Bristol Township Commissioner Harold Lefcourt; our next-door neighbors at the time, Lewis and Beatrice Wechsler and their family; our attorney Samuel Snipes; and the regional head of the AFL-CIO (I'm sorry, I can't remember his name) for what they all did for the Myers family.

When I was invited back to Levittown in 1999 for the fiftieth anniversary of Levittown, Mayor Samuel Fenton and the citizens of Levittown welcomed me with open arms. I'll never forget them.

Every so often over the years we were interviewed about our story. John D. Mullane was one of the local reporters, and he talked to his classmate, Mayor Fenton, about inviting me back. He has become a good friend.

In 1999 I joined a local writers' group in York, Pennsylvania, and that's where I met Therese Boyd. She led the class and expressed interest in seeing my manuscript. She encouraged me to have it published. But the final link came from an unexpected place. Deb Gogniat and I attend the same church. She mentioned the manuscript to her husband, Don, who then brought it to the attention of the York County Heritage Trust, where he was a board member. Through Therese's editorial efforts, the Trust agreed to publish the manuscript, and for that I thank them.

I finished writing what would become chapters one through twelve in the early 1960s and it remains unchanged today, with the exception of a few editorial notes. The introduction and chapter thirteen were added for publication.

Finally, I have to thank my family. Without my husband's assistance and support, I never would have been able to do this. He was the kind of person who never said no. I miss him every day. I dedicate this book to Bill and our children.

Daisy D. Myers
2005

Introduction

> Tonight we want to welcome back a hero. A hero is a person admired for qualities and deeds, and tonight a true hero stands in front of you—Mrs. Daisy Myers—a person of distinguished bravery, the principal figure in a story. She endured the worst kind of humiliation—racism. For that we are truly sorry.

I listened to Bristol Township Mayor Sam Fenton speak that cold night in December 1999 at the tree-lighting ceremony in Levittown, Pennsylvania. Despite the bright Christmas lights, the crowds of people, and the music in the air, for me it was a sobering time. I had very mixed feelings about returning to the place where my family and I had suffered so much. I was happy to be there, yet I was sad, too. I was welcomed so warmly I could hardly feel alone, and yet I wished my husband and best friend, Bill (who had passed twelve years before), was there by my side.

> Each year a senior is picked to light the holiday tree. To show our hospitality, this year we have asked Mrs. Myers if she would do us the honor.

I hadn't had much time to think about the invitation before it was issued. Less than a month before, my friend John Mullane, a reporter for the *Bucks County Courier Times,* had been discussing the fiftieth anniversary of Levittown with local officials and suggested that I be named to the anniversary celebration committee for 2002. When John mentioned my name, Mayor Fenton, who had been born two years after we moved to Levittown, didn't know who I was or what John was talking about. When he learned what had happened, he was shocked. He had trouble believing the story at first, but then decided that the town should make an effort at amends. I was surprised when John called me with the invitation.

> Tonight we want to welcome her and her family back with open arms and show her everyone is welcome in Bristol Township. We want to try to ease the pain of some of her past and give her new memories to live with and take with her back to York. We hope the new memories help erase away some of the old ones.

I was escorted to the ceremony by Police Captain Herb Phillips and Fire Marshal Ed Cooper in a police car with the sirens wailing and lights flashing. They had offered to come pick me up in York, about two hours west of Levittown in south central Pennsylvania, but I assured them I could drive myself. I met them at a turnpike exit, and they escorted me to the ceremony at the township building.

> The tree will serve as a reminder that what happened in the past cannot be tolerated or accepted. What is happening here tonight is the welcome she should have received long ago.

After Mayor Fenton made his speech, I flipped the switch to light the sixteen-foot blue spruce named "Miss Daisy." We then went inside the township building for a tour of the senior center and had some refreshments. Everyone was so nice to me. Some people even asked for my autograph.

One person who really touched me was Janet Sarver. She handed me a letter with a short story she had written for a creative writing class. Janet was six-and-a-half years old when we moved to Levittown. Her letter says, "I really wanted you to know what an impact that whole situation made on my life, too...What I experienced back then as a child has made me the person I am today...I hope the pain caused by the people of Levittown is gone." The Myerses weren't the only people affected by the events of 1957.

My visit gave me a chance to return to my old neighborhood and my former home on Deepgreen Lane in the Dogwood Hollow section of Levittown. Jeanette Harris, the current owner of the house, tearfully embraced and welcomed me. She said she was honored to meet me. Mrs. Harris is fully aware of the historical aspect of her house. She has set aside a section of her living room with a little museum dedicated to the Levittown incident, where she keeps framed news articles and other documents of 1957.

As I toured the house, memories flooded back. I could see Lynda in her crib, the boys in their bunk bed, and the little dog running through the house. The visit brought sad memories to mind, too, but what happened to me and to my family prepared us for who we are now--stronger human beings. Love is powerful, and the hug Mrs. Harris gave me was so helpful in making new, positive memories.

At the opening of the tree-lighting ceremony that cold December of 1999, the Reverend Mel Howard, a former township official, said, "I'm hoping what happens here tonight is a rebirth, not only in the township, but in the country and in the nation." I believe as human beings we are obligated to respect the rights of others, and this was expressed in words and actions at this ceremony. On this night love had conquered evil. Good people do exist.

Daisy D. Myers
2005

Chapter 1
Moving Day

Tuesday, August 13, 1957. We were all up early because the moving van was due at eight o'clock. Excitement had been building for months. Our long-awaited baby girl had arrived, and now we were moving. In his good, husbandly way, Bill was busy with the boys, helping our four-year-old William ready himself and keeping Stephen, the three-year-old, in line.

Even baby Lynda seemed to know it was a memorable day. Here she was exactly one month old on the same day we were moving to 43 Deepgreen Lane, Dogwood Hollow, Levittown, Pennsylvania. The coincidence seemed significant. Could it be luck—good or bad? Bill and I had no idea that morning what the next twelve hours would bring.

Our family had outgrown our house in Bloomsdale, an integrated community of over two hundred homes, which is, in fact, almost surrounded by Levittown. Three years ago we had been happy to move into this brand-new house, but now we needed another bedroom to separate the girl from the boys. While we didn't mind the attached homes in Bloomsdale—in units of four and five—we really wanted a single-family residence with more yard space.

Although our address would change with the move, we expected our lives would be about the same. After all, we were moving less than a mile from the old residence. We would still live in Bristol Township, Bucks County. We would still patronize the Levittown Shop-a-rama for most of our purchases.

In many ways, we already felt identified with Levittown. We had friends there and other close ties to the community. As a member of the recreation board, I attended social functions in and about Levittown with Bill. I was a member of the Levittown League of Women Voters and participated in discussion groups held at various homes in Levittown. While taking extension courses conducted by Temple University, I rode back and forth to classes with Levittown friends who were classmates. These connections encouraged and broadened our social contacts long before there was any thought of moving from Bloomsdale.

But we needed a larger place. The cheerful, pink, three-bedroom ranch house on the corner of Deepgreen and Daffodil Lanes in Levittown had everything we could want. Bill was particularly happy about the new garage. We had never had one before, and this one was extra large. The previous owner had built it after converting the carport into an enclosed playroom. In the rear of the playroom was a laundry, another good feature for a family with three small children. The lawn was unkempt when we looked at the house, but I knew Bill would make it attractive and the children would enjoy the ample play space. They had been cramped by the small yard in Bloomsdale. It seemed that Levittown was ideal!

For two days before we moved in, Bill and I worked in our new home, washing windows, scrubbing and waxing the floors, cleaning, and painting. We wondered what the neighbors were thinking as they saw us going in and out, but no one approached us and we kept ourselves busy.

On Tuesday morning the moving van arrived at the Bloomsdale house promptly—almost on the second. Once the van backed up to the door, the word spread among neighbors that we were moving. We had talked very little, except to close friends, about our move. Not that we wanted to be secretive, but Bill and I had agreed to keep our plans to ourselves as much as possible. We were nearly convinced that nothing would happen when we moved, but we still tried to play it safe.

Over the previous months, we had spent many hours talking about the implications of what we were about to do. We knew, like everyone else did, that the new suburb called Levittown, "the most perfectly planned community in America," was supposed to be lily-white and, as far as we could tell, the builder, Levitt & Sons, intended to keep it that way. They did not hide their policy of selling their new homes only to whites. Lawsuits had been lost by Negroes trying to buy new homes in both the New York and Pennsylvania Levittowns.[1] But we also knew that, in theory—if not in fact, any American was free to purchase a home anywhere if he could pay the purchase price.

We did not see any advantage in trying to prepare the community in advance. No other family had to do this before moving. The kind of preparations we had experienced or heard about had not convinced us it was a good idea. We had considered seeking advice from the human relations group but decided against it.

Our friends in Levittown were aware of the potential for trouble if we moved into Levittown. We had talked with them, trying to estimate community reaction. Some of those conversations, as we examined the pros and cons, were rather pleasant intellectual exercises. But something was missing from our mental gymnastics. We didn't take fully into account the prejudices of so many Americans—those silly enough to let skin color cause them to reject other human beings.

Levittown was labeled the fastest growing city in the world. The houses were built at an average of two hundred a week, using Levitt's on-site assembly line construction system with non-union labor. We should have known that this was a vast new community where Americans with as many grades of prejudice as liberalism lived. Since it was a northern city, we did not expect it to react the way a southern community might if a Negro family moved in. I wish we had been wiser. We might have realized that some of the seventy thousand Levittowners had made hurried flights to this suburban community, fleeing from the integrating neighborhoods of Philadelphia, seventeen miles to the south. How wise must a Negro family be? Must we be experts in human relations simply because we need a larger home for our growing family? Even today, at this writing, Levittown's population is still only 3 percent nonwhite.[2]

We didn't think moving from Bloomsdale to Levittown required that kind of foresightedness and preparation. We confidently, or naively, thought that we were the "right kind of family" to make the move—whatever that meant.

Our neighbors in Bloomsdale hated to see us go, and we hated leaving. We had tried to be good citizens in Bloomsdale. Bill had worked hard as leader and organizer of the Civic Association; it had given both of us much satisfaction. He helped many of our neighbors, both Negro and white, who had problems trying to persuade the builder to correct construction flaws in their homes, such as defective heating systems and warping windows. I had participated in charity work, knocking on many doors collecting money for various funds, such as polio, the Red

---

[1] In 1955 the NAACP filed suit against Levitt & Sons and federal government housing officials "seeking to force sale of homes...to Negroes. The action was dismissed at U.S. District Court in Philadelphia." See "Levittown Home of Negro Stoned: Police Guard to Prevent Incidents in Former All-White Town," Aug. 14, 1957, clipping from author's files; J. D. Mullane, "Exhibit Recalls Clashes in Summer of 1957," *Bucks County Courier Times*, January 3, 2002.

[2] *Editor's note*: According to the 2000 U.S. Census, only 3 percent of Levittown's population is African American. J. D. Mullane, "Exhibit Recalls Clashes in Summer of 1957," *Bucks County Courier Times*, January 3, 2002.

Cross, and the Levittown Public Library. I also made some political calls. During the summer, I was playground supervisor, appointed by the recreation board.

Bill and I tried to help our community in any way we could. A commercial amusement park was planned adjacent to Bloomsdale, which we felt would threaten the residential nature of the neighborhood. We worked successfully with our neighbors to prevent its construction. We couldn't always help those who asked, however. Once a lady came to me wanting help to get a church started; I must say, I couldn't help her.

Now we were moving, and our neighbors were saying goodbye as though we were going too far to see them again. The five of us piled into our automobile that morning and headed for Levittown with the moving van trailing us.

It must have been about 10:30 a.m. when we got to the house. The streets seemed so quiet. I saw two children playing on the sidewalk. In almost every backyard, clothes hung on the lines. The August sun was bright. It was hot and humid, but looking back, I think I felt a breeze. I know it was one of the hottest days in my memory. The usually beautiful, spacious lawns were scorched brown from lack of rain.

The four moving men busied themselves bringing in the furniture. We had packed some of the breakables separately, like lamps and dishes—and a set of sherbet glasses I valued—and brought them in the car. While Bill unloaded the car and directed the men where to put the furniture, I changed the baby and introduced the boys to their new home. Lynda wasn't much trouble—she was in the sleeping stage then. The boys wanted to go out, but I kept them in to avoid the heat.

We were engrossed in the chores of a new home when a knock sounded at the door. It was about noon. I remember because I was watching the clock—the movers worked by the hour and I was checking the time.

I answered the door. It was the mailman.

"May I speak to the owner?" he said.

"I am the owner," I replied.

He stepped back. The look on his face was one of fright—as if he had seen a ghost. He stuttered, "You—you the owner?"

"That's right," I said.

With a limp hand, he handed me the letter and left.

"Did you see how he looked?" I asked Bill. "He looked ill." We discussed it. Why had he knocked in the first place? It was not a registered or special delivery letter—only a business letter from our lawyer.

By this time the moving men were finished, so Bill paid them and they left. The Myers family was officially moved in.

I don't remember how long it was after the mailman left, but it seemed like only a matter of minutes before we noticed a group of three or four people gathered at a house diagonally across the street from ours. Over time other small groups assembled here and there—all on the south side of the street. We noticed a man going from house to house with a paper in his hand. "They must be getting up a petition," one of us said to the other.

The telephone rang. I answered and this lady frantically said, "I will not let my children drink chocolate milk again as long as I live." She hung up. To this day, every time I pour a glass of chocolate milk, I think about that call.

The telephone wires must have been busy, for it seemed all the neighborhood men had come home for lunch, which was unusual. Maybe the mailman had passed the word to the wives, and the wives had passed it to their husbands on the job. (That's not all we think the mailman had to do with our troubles—but that comes later.)

After about an hour, the streets were clear again, except for some children playing. They were white children, of course. The husbands were back on the jobs, I suppose, and the wives back at their housework. But they still might have been busy circulating the news of the Myerses' move or trying to catch a glimpse of us from their windows.

As I look back on that noonday gathering, I realize something significant. The groups had all formed in front of what we would later learn were the unfriendly homes.

Bill and I talked about what had happened. "Do you think there will be any trouble?" I asked.

"Oh, they just came for curiosity," Bill said. He was optimistic—or trying to be.

At any rate, there was no need at that time to entertain serious doubts. About midafternoon, our many Levittown friends started coming in to welcome us and help with the unpacking. One of them brought a big lunch for the family—an assortment of sandwiches, cake, cold drinks, and milk for the kids. It was everything we needed. We fed the kids, and Bill and I planned to eat later.

We told our friends about the mailman incident and the excitement that followed. One of them brought in the afternoon *Levittown Times and Bristol Courier*, which had a story about our move. It was a short item on an inside page—no bold type or anything to attract unusual attention. It read:

> **FIRST NEGRO FAMILY MOVES INTO LEVITTOWN**
> The first Negro family to buy a Levittown house moved into the Dogwood Hollow section this morning. Mr. and Mrs. William Myers Jr. moved here with their three children, William III, 4; Stephen, 3; and Lynda, one month.
>
> Formerly residents of Bloomsdale Gardens, the couple moved to the area two and a half years ago from York, Pa.
>
> Mr. Myers, who is an engineer, is employed by C.V. Hill and Co. in Trenton, N.J., in the refrigerator-testing laboratory. He is a World War II veteran.

The newspaper always comes off the press in the early afternoon. We learned later that the switchboard was immediately swamped with calls about the story.

Despite the midday incident and the news story, we kept calm—or tried to. We should have turned to the lunch waiting for us, but instead we resumed work. We never did get to eat that lunch. In fact, we wouldn't have a real meal in that house for several weeks.

Bill and I seemed to be doing a pretty good job of acting normal, and we decided it was safe to let the boys play outside. Lynda was no bother. All she wanted was her milk or a dry diaper.

About 4:30 trouble began to brew. At first, small groups of three and four persons began to congregate, just as they had at noon. Knots of people gathered directly across the street from our house and on the street that ran along the east side of our house. The knots turned into groups and gradually grew into crowds.

Within an hour automobiles were creeping bumper to bumper down our street. I'd never seen anything like it, except maybe for rush hour on a busy New York street or a crowd leaving a ballpark. Brakes screeched frightfully. Drivers, moving slowly, stopped suddenly to stare and jammed traffic behind them. Some men stood around passively with their hands in their pockets, but others gestured vigorously as they talked with hateful expressions. People seemed either upset or curious but mostly under control. As they moved closer and tempers rose, we could hear their rumbling voices through our open windows.

By this time, we realized that the newspaper article had probably attracted more attention than the editors had anticipated. In less time than seemed possible, we'd become a top story for area newsmen. At about 7:30 p.m. the press began arriving. Flashbulbs were popping outside, and we were having our moments on the inside. In due respect for the press, I'll say that they held off from trying to get to us, in the beginning at least.

One character did get inside, but he wasn't a newsman, just someone whose boldness was, doubtlessly, boosted by his drinking. When I first saw him, he was standing near the doorway talking to Bill. Some of our friends had returned for the evening, and they tried to help Bill handle the intruder, who was doing his best to interrogate us. "All I want to know is who sold this house to you people? How much did you pay for it? What right do you have to come? I just want to find the people who sold it. Just tell me what their names are. When did you make settlement?" he tried to question Bill.

Bill kept calm and told him, "It's all part of the public record. Check it in Doylestown." That's the county seat for Bucks County.

Somehow Bill and our friends finally got the intruder out of the house. Once he was outside, the mob surrounded him. They wanted to get the real lowdown from the man who knew. I suppose they were disappointed in the information he'd gotten.

Some of our friends went out and tried to calm the people. The crowd thinned a little, but others insisted, "Something is going to happen…I'm sticking around to see it." Some people parked their cars instead of just moving through, but the heavy traffic continued. The crowd grew and became louder. We telephoned the local police, the township manager, and the Pennsylvania State Police again and again. The state police said, "It's up to the local police." The local police said, "The situation is being taken care of." But it wasn't.

Tension mounted both outside and inside. We had intended to return to Bloomsdale for the night, but we didn't feel safe leaving our new home with the large crowds outside. We had always planned on staying in our old home for the first few days after moving. We had not yet moved our beds from Bloomsdale so that we could sleep there until the faulty oil tank was repaired at the Levittown house. However, I must admit that while this gave us a valid reason for leaving, I expect we would have found some other place to rest that night anyway. Our departure would later be badly misrepresented.

As I recall, one newsman did get into the house before we left and talked to us. He was decent to us and asked a lot of questions. He wanted to get a complete story, and we felt he was trying to do his job. The next day his story carried the name of the previous owner who sold us the house. I believe that was the only story to give that information in the beginning. We wish it had not appeared, but there was nothing to be done about it. That, too, was part of the public record.

As the sun began to fade, we asked ourselves, "Will this ever end?" It was then that two agitators arrived in front of our home. One a short, thickly built man of about forty-five, drinking beer from a can, and the other a tall white-haired man of about fifty-five, began talking of burning, dynamiting, "blasting them to bits." They said, "Let's do it," but they only kept talking about it.

The police finally arrived and began to ticket parked automobiles. Within a few minutes, there wasn't a car on the streets. The people scrambled and the cars moved in a hurry. At this point, the crowds respected the police.

We left the house about 8:00 that night amid flashing bulbs and grinding cameras. Nobody knows exactly how big the mob was, but I'd say it was in the hundreds.

The drive back to Bloomsdale was one of the longest trips I have ever taken to cover so short a distance. Bill and I were disillusioned. I wondered what the experience would mean to the children and consoled myself that little Lynda, resting quietly in my arms as we rode, would not know what we had just experienced. But what about the boys? Would this be their childhood's earliest remembered experience? I prayed that it would not be.

We'd never appreciated the safety and security of the old home as we did when we entered that night. Despite the bareness and disorder, it was still home.

With sighs of relief we relaxed in bed. But instead of sleep reviving me, wonder, worry, tension, fatigue, even fear, kept me awake—and thinking. What would this controversy do to Bill? Could he keep his job? One advantage of the new location was its closeness to his work. What about the next day when we would go back? Could we stay and know the happiness we'd known in Bloomsdale? Bill didn't go to work the next day, so I was saved the fear of being without him the second day. He'd taken his vacation to do the moving.

Why were the crowds at our home? Are we different from the average family that moved to Levittown? Are we immune to the yearning for a little suburban home with green grass and flowers all around? Do we love our children less than they do? Are we sick and tired of ghettos? Do we have the right to choose a neighborhood or do the neighbors have a right to choose us? Have they come to tell us where we shall or shall not live? Aren't we human? To the mob we were not—according to their standards. What hope could we have that their distorted values would change? And, was it our responsibility to bring about the conversion? I didn't think so. I was more concerned with the responsibilities a mother feels for those she loves and those who love her.

Did we not, I asked myself, as an American Negro family have a legal and moral right to live in a place of our own choosing? What of the American ideals of justice and equality? As I lay in bed, my mind drifted back to quieter times.

Chapter 2
My Early Years

In the security of our Bloomsdale home that night, I thought about our lives. What had the years made of us since my early days in Virginia and Bill's in Pennsylvania?

I was born on February 10, 1925, in Richmond, Virginia, the only child of Myers and Lottie Dailey. Our neighborhood was known as Navy Hill, or Jackson Ward, one of the major Negro sections of the city. We lived just a few blocks from the Negro business district and Slauter's Hotel, which was famous as a stopping place for Negro travelers. Most of the neighborhood residents were "middle class" and owned their homes. We had teachers, mail carriers, and a good number of professional people, like doctors and lawyers. Most of the professional men had offices in their homes, mainly because no downtown office space was available to Negroes.

Our home was only one block from the birthplace of the famed dancer Bill "Bojangles" Robinson. I remember clearly one of his visits back home to dedicate a stoplight in Jackson Ward, although I'm not quite sure why a traffic signal justified such a major celebration. Today there is a statue of tennis star Arthur Ashe, who grew up in a house I used to pass every day on my way to high school.

My father worked for the Richmond, Fredericksburg & Potomac Railroad. We did everything as a family. All the day's problems were solved somehow over our family meals. On Sunday evenings, we gathered around the radio to listen to "Inner Sanctum." We traveled a lot because my father's job granted free family passes to ride the train anywhere we wanted to go.

My parents were deeply religious people. Father was a deacon in the church for over forty years, and Mother held just about all the positions traditionally open to women. I think we were present as a family every time the doors opened. I would not say they were rigid parents, but they held to the "old school of discipline," and that was—I used to think—rather strict. My mother had a certain "look" to let me know when I was misbehaving, and that was enough to change my behavior without question.

Education was a priority in my home. Because my birth date was not in the "early" category, I was not admitted to elementary school on my first try but had to wait a year. We were disappointed because I knew I was prepared. I knew my name, address, parents' names, colors, numbers, and the alphabet.

When I did enter school, there was no cafeteria, gymnasium, or auditorium. We were dismissed for an hour to return home for lunch. Our exercise classes were taken in the classroom, along with art and other extracurricular activities. I sat up front in all my classes because I was nearsighted and liked being close to the teacher. I wanted to be a teacher when I grew up and even played school with my friends whenever I could.

Once we were in high school, we ate in a cafeteria and had a gym, auditorium, and library. I enjoyed every year of it, although I couldn't seem to get old fast enough. In my senior year, I was chosen most popular senior by my classmates. I was flattered and floated on cloud nine for a while.

And yet, my life in Richmond was all Jim Crow. In public places, gatherings, and conveyances we were segregated. I attended segregated schools, rode in the back of the trolley, could not eat in most restaurants or sit at food counters. There were "colored" and "white" signs all over the place. The phrase "separate but equal" was heard a lot. We had to use different toilets, libraries, and drinking fountains, and take whatever jobs the white man thought appropriate for us.

I graduated from high school at sixteen and entered Virginia Union College the same year, majoring in sociology and minoring in education. When I received my bachelor's degree four years later, I left home for my first teaching assignment at a high school in Amelia, Virginia, about thirty-five miles south of Richmond. Because there were no student-teaching programs for college students at that time, we learned "on the job" by teaching for a year in the rural areas.

Considering what most Negro school situations in small southern communities were like, Amelia's school was not the worst, but it was far from the best. My schedule was a backbreaker. I taught some of nearly everything in the curriculum: social studies, mathematics, English, and physical education. I also coached the basketball team for girls and the cheering squad.

That one year of teaching convinced me that I needed to prepare myself better—and to seek something better. In 1947 I left my beautiful home state to move to New York with two girlfriends for graduate studies at New York University.

My parents were very concerned for my safety and lectured me carefully before I left Richmond. They told me to be cautious, warning me that New York City was "like a Venus flytrap." I heard, "Be sure to do this," and "Be sure not to do that," over and over again.

I arrived in New York in the morning. What a city! I thought. The streets were filled with people going to and from work. I had never seen such a sight in all my life. I gazed up at the towering buildings that seemed to touch the sky. The honking of horns, the airbrakes of the trucks, the big double-decker buses, the smaller buses, the chatter of people, all added to the excitement. Here I was in the "big city." I was fascinated by the size and swiftness of everything. After all those years in quiet Virginia, it was like raising a shade to let the light in.

Long before I was able to settle into the routine of study, I was making contrasts between the city I had left and the one that now offered thrilling new challenges. Often, as I wandered through New York's streets, I wondered why Negroes there seemed so different from those in Richmond. I was struck by the fact that those in the North seemed so much more aggressive and interested in civic affairs and civil rights than my people back home. I am proud to be a Virginian, but in Richmond, I thought, they seemed to lack the desire to change existing conditions. For example, some of my friends who were schoolteachers would register but not bother to vote.

All I had ever known was the South, but I began to wonder if racial segregation had handicapped me. On many occasions, I felt that I was being treated differently because I was a Negro. I was more suspicious than I should have been. It was a defensive attitude I had acquired, a survival state of mind. The fact that Negroes live in a segregated world does not mean they live in either a simple or a happy world.

I had not thought about the race problem while I was growing up; it had little or no meaning to me then. But living in Virginia is like working deep inside a coal mine. You don't know what's going on until you come up for a breath of fresh air—if you can get up.

New York was that breath of fresh air to me. Here I saw Negroes seated on buses from the front to the rear. Negroes with skilled positions worked in nearly all fields. Negro artists and musicians displayed their talents before mixed audiences without incident. I sat in mixed classes at New York University without any trouble, except within myself. I could hardly believe my own eyes as I saw white students to the right and left of me. I asked myself, "If it works here, why not everywhere?" It was like a Promised Land.

I began to realize that Virginia had restricted me and all other Negroes unmercifully. And yet people often claimed, "The Virginia Negro seemed happiest." I wonder. Many of my friends back home were discontented, even bitter, but restrictions limited free expression. They said, "What's the use?" Others felt it was "home," despite the shortcomings. Others might have wanted to leave, but that opportunity never knocked. Who would listen sympathetically to their pleas? Who would point the way to an escape hatch?

I often wonder if my parents ever considered leaving the South. I don't remember that we ever discussed the point specifically, but I'm sure the circumstances of their lives discouraged such thoughts. My father always had what was considered a good job in terms of what was available to Negroes and the security of being able to keep it. By the time he retired, after fifty-six years, he was what the railroad folks know as a "cooper," the man responsible for handling damaged freight. Although my father worked for the railroad longer than his boss, his long years of service did not bring promotion to a higher job. The boss had to be a white man, although Father may have been otherwise better qualified. Two of his bosses retired during his fifty-six years. He had reached retirement age, too, but refused to do so until he was disabled.

Despite all of the disadvantages the South imposed on Negroes, I have always been thankful that my father had a job that assured us a bit of economic security and a comfortable standard of living. While both of my parents were deeply religious and thankful for the blessings they received, this did not blind them to injustices. They voted regularly and Mother always kept track of their poll taxes.[3] They often urged other Negro friends and relatives to pay the poll tax and vote. Many times my parents used their automobile to furnish transportation so others could vote. Their membership in the National Association for the Advancement of Colored People was never neglected. Maybe it was not the same kind of allegiance they held to their church, but it was nearly the same.

My trip away from home was destined to have great consequences for me, far more significant than I could have imagined. Although I had been in New York once before, as a child, I did not remember it. This time I had an opportunity to fulfill some ambitions, to experience what life could be like for Negroes outside of Jim Crow.

During the year I studied in New York City, I also worked part-time as a circulation clerk in a large publishing firm. I worked with whites and Negroes with no racial incidents ever. We all worked side by side, had lunch together, and sometimes visited in the evenings. One Negro foreman had more white than Negro workers under his supervision.

---

[3]*Editor's note:* Between 1889 and 1910, southern states used the payment of poll taxes as a prerequisite for voting, which kept many blacks and poor whites from being able to vote. Some of these taxes were abolished by the 1940s. The 24th Amendment to the U.S. Constitution was passed in 1964, which disallowed the poll tax as a requirement for voting in federal elections (see www.infoplease.com).

In 1948 I had to return to Virginia due to illness in my family. I enrolled at Hampton Institute in Hampton, Virginia, for the summers of 1949 and 1950 to continue my education. In the fall of my second year, I took a teaching job at Phoenix High School on the Hampton College campus. It was there that I met, fell in love, and decided to marry Bill Myers.

Bill grew up in York, Pennsylvania. He had attended York High School, where he was the first and only Negro member in the York High School band. Since he played clarinet, his friends called him "Benny," for Benny Goodman. In 1942 Bill left York to attend Hampton on a basketball scholarship. As it was for most young men at the time, Bill's study at Hampton was interrupted by World War II. He served in the Army Quartermaster Corps for two years and spent time in the European theater. He earned the rank of staff sergeant before discharge, and then returned to Hampton to complete his bachelor's degree in electricity in 1948. The college hired him immediately upon graduation. When I met him he was teaching courses in electricity at Hampton and working on the college maintenance staff.

While we were dating, Bill and I often rode in his car to the banks of the Chesapeake Bay in Newport News, Virginia. We would sit together, watching and listening to the waves as they lashed the shoreline. We talked, joked, and threw rocks in the water. When the subject of marriage came up, Bill told me almost immediately, "I certainly do not intend to live in the South and subject my children to its discrimination."

Bill had never adjusted to segregation. His mother had visited Bill at Hampton only once—her first time in the South. She sat beside a white man on a trolley, and he tried to push her off the seat. Humiliated, she swore she would never return and even refused to visit Bill as long as he stayed at Hampton. She didn't even want to come to Richmond for our wedding, but she finally relented.

Bill and I were married in December 1950 at my home in Richmond and set up housekeeping in one of the temporary housing projects at Hampton. We talked about a permanent location in the South, but I got nowhere with Bill. I wanted to be near my family and friends. I was familiar with Richmond and all it had to offer; to me, it was a warm and caring community.

While Bill may not have known a lot about the region, the little he did know he didn't like. Although we were living cheaply in the project apartments, we wanted a home of our own, and Bill would not think of buying a house there. He also knew he would not be admitted to an electrical union anywhere in the South. When the school term ended in 1951, we moved to Bill's hometown of York, Pennsylvania, seeking a freer life.

Chapter 3
Above the Mason-Dixon Line

Because I'd lived in New York City for a while, I was naive enough to assume that all the northern states were similar in their treatment of minority groups. When Bill and I were dating he talked about York so much—he saw York as warm, friendly, and hospitable. I had never heard of this place and finally asked him if he meant New York City. He answered emphatically, "No. I'm talking about York, Pa." So I expected York to offer us much in the way of a rich and full life and went there with enthusiasm. Here, I told myself, we would have a fighting chance at contentment.

York, with a population of about 60,000 in 1950, is twenty-eight miles south of Harrisburg and ninety miles west of Philadelphia. It is only a forty-five minute ride to Baltimore. Surely a town so well located and so accessible to other great cities must be ideal, I thought. The streets in the central part of the city bear such names as King, Queen, Duke, Princess, and George, and the city itself was named for the English "York." The first settlers were chiefly German, English, and Scotch-Irish. York was also a big commercial and manufacturing community.

Our first brush with the sore of racial segregation came when we set out to find housing. We wanted to buy, so we were fairly selective. Two houses were considered: one of them I did not like, and the other was located on a block that, except for one Negro family, was white. The real estate agent said he was sorry, but he could not sell to Negroes. Here again was this contagious, malignant form of racial prejudice.

Fortunately Bill's mother knew some influential people in town, and we were able to buy a house at 45 East Maple Street. We then discovered that the people next door were the ones who had objected. Once we were moved in, a next-door neighbor came over and knocked. He hollered, "Who are my neighbors?"

Bill answered, "I am, come on upstairs."

When he reached the top of the stairway and saw it was Bill, he said, "Oh, it's you, Benny. We didn't know who it was."

What he was saying was that they objected to most Negroes, but Bill might be all right as a neighbor since they had been buddies in school some years back. They laughed and talked of old times for hours. Then he left and brought his entire household over. Among them was his sister-in-law who had earlier ranted and raved, banged her screen door, and threw a tin pail to the ground about twenty times. Now, in our home, she was calmer and said, "I'm sorry, but we didn't know who was moving in here."

After I had gotten to know her more intimately, she tried to explain her prejudiced feelings. She told me that she had been brought up in a Negro neighborhood where her parents had a corner store. Negro customers provided her family's livelihood. She was born there, played, and ate with Negro children and yet later, as a woman, she had felt "superior" to her former friends of another race. The constant day-to-day contacts made her bend somewhat, but she still had a less-than-positive attitude.

The next fall, with teaching still in my blood, I was hired as a substitute teacher at the two all-black elementary schools in York. Integration was taking over at the time, but it moved slowly. That same year, 1951, black children began attending all-white schools, but full integration wasn't complete until 1955.

While I was a substitute teacher I kept looking for a full-time job. I noticed a news article announcing plans for new low-rent housing. They needed a supervisor, family interviewer, investigators, and a stenographer. Applications could be placed by telephone, the story said. With my background in sociology, I thought a job in public housing would be ideal, so I telephoned the office and applied. I was told that I'd be notified to come for a personal interview. After many weeks, I was called and given an appointment.

I arrived promptly for the interview and approached the supervisor. She looked up, shocked to see a Negro applicant. A moment of silence followed and, finally, nervously adjusting her eyeglasses, she said, "You—are you Mrs. Myers?"

I said, "Surely."

As the interview started, I began to feel I was fired before I was hired. She admitted my qualifications were good, but told me it was a question of "whether I am allowed to hire a Negro or not."

While I answered, "I understand," actually, I did not. Such are the conflicts a Negro must experience far too often in our unequal system in some locales.

The supervisor said, "If at all possible, I will call you by telephone." I thanked her and left feeling defeated and dejected. But in a matter of days, she called and told me to report to work. I thought I must be dreaming and counted the hours and minutes until Bill would come home from work so that I could tell him the good news.

On my first day in the office, my supervisor and I got to know each other better. She had been a social worker on an Indian reservation in California and had moved east because of her health. In one conversation she opened up the race question and confided that she had gone to bat for me to obtain the position. Why? The housing authority, consisting of a board of older, conservative men, had been reluctant to hire a Negro. Our relationship in the months that followed was very positive.

This job opened my eyes to some people's living conditions. Although I had seen the rural South, I did not realize what a sheltered life I had led until my job as a family interviewer took me to some homes in the York area. As many as five, six, or seven people were living in two-room apartments. Outhouses were prevalent instead of bathrooms. Many homes lacked running water and electricity.

My warm relationship with my supervisor continued, but prejudice reared its head when applicants started coming to the office. One day an older white man, half deaf and bent with age, walked in and spoke loudly, "They tell me niggers gonna live side by side with white folks out there, and I ain't filling out no forms 'til I find this out."

My supervisor answered him calmly and politely, "There are many people of different races in this world, and some day they will all learn to live side by side if America is to be the democratic country she set out to be."

Months later, when the supervisor had to leave the job because of poor health, I was made acting supervisor. I was next in line for the promotion. I worked hard and, in my own mind, anticipated the day I would become supervisor.

At least I did not have to go on very long living in that dream world. Before too much time passed, the executive director came to me and said, "Mrs. Myers, a new lady will be in to take over the job as supervisor. I'd like you to teach her everything you know. You see, this lady has no experience in this field but has worked as an accountant."

As I think back on it, "experience" was the primary consideration when I applied, but now, in her case, it was only secondary because she was white. I decided to resign and gave thirty days' notice. The director pleaded day after day for me to remain. He said he knew how I felt and that it was not his fault, but he had orders from those "higher up." He even offered to increase my salary, but it all fell on deaf ears. I quit and went back to teaching.

While we lived in York, we started our family. It seemed like we had waited such a long time because we had both wanted a child right after we married. When I became pregnant for the first time, we were overjoyed. My husband put his order in for a boy because he wanted someone to play sports with him. I wanted a girl, but we both agreed we would be happy with a normal, healthy baby. Bill's "order" was filled when William III was born December 1, 1952. Because neither of us had been around infants before, Bill and I grew into our roles as parents. We both did what had to be done, and I could always count on Bill as a helper.

While our family life was happy, employment was not as easy to find as we hoped. Most of Bill's childhood classmates and friends had left York by the time we moved there. Bill had enjoyed his hometown as a child and teenager, but as a man, he found it had little to offer him with his electrical background. When he received a layoff notice, he explored the possibility of work in the Philadelphia area, and we moved there. By this time, we had become a family of four, with son Stephen born the year after William. We were still seeking the refuge that York had not provided.

We hoped that Philadelphia—the City of Brotherly Love—might bring this fulfillment. We knew something of its tradition of liberty and strong opposition to slavery before and during the Civil War. I knew, for example, that the first formal protest against slavery was made by citizens of Germantown in 1688. The first Abolitionist convention was held in Philadelphia in 1794. It had been an important center for the Underground Railroad, strongly backed by the Quakers.

William Penn had invited early settlers who had known toil, fear, and misfortune to this new land of promise, offering peace, material rewards, religious freedom, and affordable land. They braved the dangerous voyage across the Atlantic to clear the great forests of Bucks County. They moved huge rocks and fought to save their small crops from native wildlife. They dealt humanely with Indians. They triumphed, but some 270 years later, the Myerses and other Negro families had a different antagonist. Even though we were now in the North, our foe was still Jim Crow.

We took an apartment in Philadelphia and looked around for a home to purchase. Our agent told us some new houses were being built in the suburbs and that we might like to take a look at them. With little else to go on, we drove through many neighborhoods in different directions. Northeast of Philadelphia, we found Bloomsdale Gardens in Bristol, Bucks County. Bristol, with a population of more than 10,000, is the third-oldest town in Pennsylvania. It was first settled in 1697 and designated as Bucks County seat in 1705. A Friends' Meetinghouse built in 1710–14 still stands there.

Bristol was a quiet little town when we lived there, close to the new housing being built in Levittown just across the main highway. It looked like an ideal place for our growing family. We made the move to Bloomsdale Gardens.

Chapter 4
The Decision Is Made

Now we were moving again, this time to Levittown. Why, and under what circumstances, does a family decide to move to another house? But for the fact that we were leaving our home in an integrated neighborhood to move to one that wasn't, our answer would be about the same as that of thousands of other Americans who change residences each year.

I wish it could have been as simple for us as it is for most other people.

Several months before our move, we heard about the Levittown house in a casual way. Bill and I were members of an informal discussion group sponsored by the William Penn Center in Fallsington, Pennsylvania, a community near Levittown. We met in various Levittown homes. The informal discussions covered a wide range of topics including political, social, economic, and educational issues. Most of the participants were residents of Levittown. Bill and I were the only Negro members of the group.

Sometimes speakers were brought to the group, and their talks were tape-recorded for further discussion at a subsequent session. We combined some social activities with the discussion and usually had coffee and cookies at the end of an evening.

It was at one of these meetings in the early spring of 1957 that the idea of moving to Levittown was first mentioned. Someone said to Bill, "Do you know a nice Negro couple that would like to move to Levittown?" Bill's quick answer was, "No." Driving home that night, Bill told me about the remark, and we started toying with the possibility of moving there. I remember saying, "How about us?" We joked about the idea since, at the time, it seemed beyond reality. It hadn't been that long since the NAACP took the Levitt company to court and lost.

Since we were in the market for another house, however, the Levittown idea lingered. We had been looking around to see if anything was available that we could buy. We saw hundreds of homes in numerous developments about Bucks County, but we knew without asking that they were not intended for Negro buyers. We'd thought about moving back into Philadelphia and were engaged in a debate over whether we would continue as suburban residents or settle for another city apartment or one of the Philadelphia roughhouses.

Another factor that complicated the move for us was the difficulty of disposing of our house in the Bloomsdale project. It seemed like they were hard-luck houses, and the builder never did sell them all. Potential buyers did not want to move out from Philadelphia or did not want to pay $9,500 for them. If a buyer did have that much to invest, new ones were available and more attractive than the ones that had already been occupied.

Though we'd begun to think that we were stuck in the Bloomsdale house, we decided to carry the "joke" a bit further. We would ask some questions and get more details the next time the discussion group met.

When the question was raised the next time, Bill said, "Suppose we wanted to move?" The response was favorable, but for us the matter was still hypothetical, so we carefully avoided any commitment. Yet we tried to keep the issue alive and explained that a decision of that nature demanded careful consideration and ample time for deliberation.

What we didn't know at the time was that a group called the Bucks County Human Relations Council had been looking for a Negro family willing to move to

Levittown. Its interest in breaking the lily-white pattern of the project had no relation to our desire to find a good home in a desirable neighborhood where we could live a full, gratifying life.

After we had a few casual conversations during our group's social hours, someone suggested a special meeting to discuss the possibility of our moving to Levittown. Members of the discussion group made up the core of the dozen or more persons who voluntarily met. We never formally organized or picked a name, but if we had, I suppose we might have been known as the "Levittown Committee to Discuss the Successful Move-in of a Negro Family." The emphasis would be on the word "discuss" since we put long hours of talk into the matter.

While the group was informal and without official sponsorship, several key persons participated in their individual capacities. They were affiliated with the William Penn Center, human relations organizations, and a religious organization. There were no local ministers present nor did any religious organization have an official relationship to the early discussions.

The group had at least four meetings, and we were put through the third degree answering questions—some were relevant, but others seemed stupid. We did most of the talking. I finally said that we were only ordinary people—we had not invented anything or created sensations or been in any trouble. They pried into our lives so extensively that one would wonder if they were going to give us a house instead of us having to buy it.

When we had been thoroughly examined and cross-examined, the conversations dealt at length with the possibility of trouble that might happen. It was generally agreed that there might be some resistance, but it was expected to come chiefly from the immediate neighborhood. There was concern about the possible action of some bigots responsible for a series of anti-Negro, anti-Semitic yellow pamphlets that had been distributed following pro-integration editorials and letters in the Levittown newspaper. It was suggested that the yellow sheets forged Jewish names to encourage anti-Semitic feeling against the leadership in the local civic association, which was mostly Jewish. It claimed that the signers supported integration. This "yellow sheet incident" had caused great concern in and about Levittown; it was a genuine hate campaign in the making.

While we heard no dissent among the group over the principal objective of getting a Negro family into Levittown, there were some differences about details. Someone suggested that a door-to-door canvass be made to determine if a Negro family would be acceptable to the neighbors. We vetoed that idea immediately. Bill and I wondered who was going to pay for the house—the neighbors or the Myerses. We have always felt that Negroes have too long been expected to ask permission for what they deserve. It seemed to us that this technique would only give the opposition a chance to organize against us. Maybe it made no difference in the end, but I am positive it would not have helped prepare the community.

Today—in the early 1960s—canvassing is done to find friendly neighbors before the minority family moves in so that, in the event of violence, there will be people to rally immediately with strong community support. Counseling is available with these friendly people and public authorities to calm racial tensions, if any, and to prevent the flight of white residents and, in so doing, promote a pattern of integration.

The conversations of early 1957 appear rather curious as I look back on them now. It appears that the idea running through the talks was that if one family moved in this vast community of seventy thousand persons, the job of integrating Levittown would be complete. Some of the folks in the group were unduly afraid that panic selling might follow our move in and wanted to be sure that the flow of Negroes would be controlled.

This point always manages to disguise the real issue involved in the process of integrating a neighborhood. Panic selling is the end result when white residents are motivated by their own prejudices. It is a simple matter for unscrupulous real estate men to magnify those fears and exploit the opportunity to make a few dollars on the sales that follow. They begin to work, bringing in as many nonwhites as possible while urging the whites to leave. This, of course, is unethical, but it gives them considerable influence in perpetuating segregation. The Negro newcomers cannot contribute to a panic situation over which they have no control. Naturally, there are many potential Negro buyers who seek a better home, and they buy where houses are available. The restrictions that prevent Negro homebuyers from competing freely in an open market often force them into ghettos.

This situation also helps support the myth that Negroes prefer to live with their own people and are, thereby, happier with the opportunity to buy into a neighborhood where Negro residents predominate. It is a fact, however, that Negroes—like all other human beings—enjoy a neighborhood where they can enjoy a normal pattern of life among people who respect them for what they are, regardless of the color of their skin. A Negro expects no more or no less of his neighbors than a person of any other race, religion, or national origin.

Another curious circumstance about Levittown, prior to our move there, is that it was already integrated in a way. So many persons of varied complexions lived there that many of its residents assumed that the color pattern had been broken earlier—and had accepted what was a fact. Among the residents were Puerto Ricans, American Indians, and Asians. Some of the couples were a mixture of Negro and white, or white and American Indian. Some of Bill's coworkers said they could not understand what the problem was—they thought Negroes had lived in Levittown all the time.

We disregarded these facts as we approached the question of moving. Somehow, ours was a special case, in the nauseating way it nearly always is when a Negro tries to break out of the stranglehold America's undemocratic pattern has on him.

Eventually it became known that a house was available; it had been unoccupied for nearly a year. By this time, we had set our minds on one of the "Jubilee" houses of Levittown because it provided the space and facilities we felt were necessary for our family. But the one we were later to consider was a ranch home, called a "Levittowner," next door to Lewis and Bev Wechsler, members of the William Penn Center group and proponents of our move to Levittown. The house seemed ideal for our growing family. At $12,000 it was within our financial range; it had been remodeled and enlarged, giving our children plenty of room to play. We wanted to make the move from Bloomsdale Gardens.

Many days passed, and some nights Bill and I found ourselves sitting on our bed discussing Levittown. The first and last question was always the kids, although Bill made me an important issue in trying to decide. How much could I take—and Bill—and the kids? We pondered these questions with our very souls.

Could we protect our children?

Taking extreme care to examine all factors and possible obstacles, we tried to reason out what we believed about our rights, what the Constitution says about "inalienable rights," and what our Christian heritage had taught us. It wasn't easy, but we held to the faith that "right" would triumph. It was not a blind faith that let us ignore the troublesome questions.

Would our children be ostracized? Would we be able to live in the home once we had purchased it? To what extent would our neighbors object? Would the developer, by some maneuvering, try to get us out? Could we live a normal, happy life in Levittown?

Our own sensitivity, sharpened by discrimination and suffering, made the questions even more agonizing. The questions seemed never ending—there were always more, more, and still more!

Even so, we came to the conclusion that a few days, or months, or years of harassment would not scar our children beyond repair. I am not nearly so certain about this now in the early 1960s as I was then. However, I hope that their youthful spirits did not register all the heartaches that could not be repulsed by their parents who had, by that time, learned the hard lessons of man's inhumanity. We were a product of the American heritage, which had taught us the evil of Jim Crow, and although we could not experience it, we knew that the better life was one without the limitations of Jim Crow.

As the weeks went on, we became more optimistic about the move. "Maybe we are crossing too many bridges before we get to them," we said. We were hopeful that the good people in Levittown favored the move of a Negro family. Without any knowledge of our plans, the local newspaper had carried several editorials on the rights of Negroes and minority groups. In February an editorial on Brotherhood Week appeared, followed by another in support of the Montgomery, Alabama, bus boycott and the work of the human relations council in Bucks County. Another editorial printed just prior to our move favored integration. The paper had consistently given liberal and favorable news coverage to the efforts of local residents who showed good will by working toward intergroup ideals or goals. Its coverage and support of the Pennsylvania Fair Employment Practices Commission bill was outstanding and helped awaken both representatives and senators to their responsibilities.

Earlier that year the editor had been chairman of a conference arranged by the American Friends Service Committee and the Human Relations Council, at which time the Reverend Ralph Abernathy of Montgomery, Alabama, was the principal speaker. About 375 people at the Faith Reformed Church heard him speak of the Montgomery protest as "a great dramatic occurrence on the American scene." Many people have associated our moving in with this meeting, but there was no relationship at all. I read about the wonderful speech in the newspaper because we could not attend personally.

In the end, the countless factors we had examined with what we thought was precision added up to a positive answer. Our friends in Levittown, who had wide contacts among the residents, began to feel sure that we would have the community's backing. We expected that the newspapers, politicians, ministers, priests, rabbis, police, and various organizations would speak on our behalf if needed. As a result, Bill and I decided affirmatively "we would move to Levittown."

Chapter 5
The First Week in Levittown

The night of retreat—away from the crowds and the reporters on our new front lawn, amid the security of our old Bloomsdale home—enabled us to recapture some of the enthusiasm we had had as we left for Levittown with our furniture. We'd not been able to sleep off all the apprehensions fomented by the previous day's experiences. In a way, we awoke on Wednesday morning with conflicted personalities. We wanted to go back to the Levittown house that we had bought and, yet, as I think back, there spilled over from my subconscious a resistance that I did not care to admit. Since I could not admit it to myself, I was restrained from putting the words into a conversation with Bill.

Though there were doubts, they had arisen without our knowing what had transpired Tuesday night after we had returned to Bloomsdale. We got a full report shortly after we arose when some friends came to tell us a story that was not reassuring. One of the mob had hurled a rock that broke our picture window facing the street on the south side of the house. Several times lit cigarettes thrown against the house nearly started a blaze in the grass, which was dried almost to a crisp by the midsummer drought.

Friends and neighbors had called the police asking for help but had been told that they "couldn't do anything until something happened." Earlier Tuesday night, before we left, the police had ticketed automobiles and cleared the streets, but the crowds returned later and the police resorted to acting as traffic officers, listening to the threats, but doing nothing. Their "do-nothing" role was, perhaps unintentionally, a tip-off to the mob that they need not fear police restrictions—that the law was on their side. Some even bragged, "The police live in Levittown, too."

According to the newspaper, about 200 people gathered that night. Agitators moved through the growing crowds, steaming them up. Women were the most vicious—using profanity and venting their emotions against us and whomever else they imagined was responsible for our move. They would spit and curse and urge the men to do something.

Telephone calls for the police started about eight o'clock, but it was about midnight before they arrived. As the situation grew increasingly acute, the police set up headquarters at the home of the township manager, which was very near our house. Once the mob turned to violence, the county sheriff and a riot squad moved into action. A three-minute deadline was set for the crowd to disperse and go home. Some moved out, but some didn't. Five of the rioters were arrested and charged with disorderly conduct. Three were teenagers who, according to court records, refused to move for the police and said things like "This is where the nigger lovers live." Their cases were sent to juvenile court. But the other two, husband and wife Howard and Agnes Bentcliffe, were in their mid-forties and for them this would be only the beginning. In later court records, their behavior that first night was described as "fairly belligerent."[4]

Though the police may have thought their action adequate for the circumstances at the moment, I feel they made a mistake by failing to charge the offenders with inciting to riot. It was a small matter for the guilty individuals to pay the ten-dollar fine for their misconduct, but the more serious charge might have averted much that followed.

---

[4] *Commonwealth of Pennsylvania v. Williams et al.*, September 1957 term.

CHAPTER 5
The First Week in Levittown

I suppose we must have gotten some consolation from the police action since we followed our original plans and returned to the house about ten o'clock on Wednesday morning. Whatever small consolation we mustered was insufficient to remove the heaviness in our hearts as we returned.

All was calm as we drove up; the streets were as clear as they had been the day before when we arrived. One might have concluded that the crisis had been short-lived. That was not the case, although it was tempting to grasp at such a hopeful conclusion. As Bill parked the car, I stared at the house and saw that the picture window had already been repaired by our friends who had managed to replace the glass that morning.

I led the Myers procession into the yard. The walkway by the window was covered with shattered glass and rocks and burned cigarettes. I looked at the replaced window and the debris, and anger stabbed me; I felt defiant. Why had this been done to an average American family? I thought we were average, despite the fact that our skins were black.

I opened the front door, and there on the floor was still more glass from the broken window and the rock that had been hurled through it. This rock, weighing less than an ounce, carried tons of hatred with it. I was afraid to let the children come into the kitchen until I could sweep it up. As I did, I thought of the woman who had committed adultery and was brought before Jesus, who said, "Let him who is without sin among you be the first to throw a stone at her."

Despite all that had happened, I hoped we could have a normal day and get some of the chores done. First, there was breakfast to be prepared. It was not an exciting one, and I know that the depression I was trying to hide was undercutting my usual enthusiasm for my family's physical welfare.

Before breakfast we cleared away flashbulbs, cigarettes, and debris left by the mob and the press the night before. Then we turned to the other tasks of housecleaning. We tried to complete some painting in the kitchen in order to be ready for wallpapering. Soon it was apparent that the telephone was competing with the housecleaning for our attention. It seemed that we were hearing from everyone I ever knew. They had all heard what had happened. Levittown, Pennsylvania, had become national news overnight. The radio was broadcasting the news, television stations flashed pictures, and the newspapers made the incident into a big story.

From nearby Morrisville, New Jersey, a woman who identified herself as white called to express disgust with what was happening. "I'm ashamed of my race," she said.

A man calling from Yuma, Arizona, said, "You may be sure that many of us are with you in your struggle against ignorant prejudice. Stick this out as long as you can for it is brave people like you who are showing the world that all men are created equal."

Another consoling call came from a fuel-oil dealer who assured us that we would get service from his company. He also expressed regret that the newspapers ignored the fact that more than fifty-five thousand Levittowners were at home sleeping peacefully while the demonstrations of five hundred were taking place.

The William Penn Center rescued us from the telephone burden by sending over teams of two ladies to accept the calls and telegrams that were pouring in. The volunteers took all messages, changing shifts every two hours throughout the day and late evening.

During the midday hours, the telephone calls—some from as far away as Nebraska—helped keep us optimistic. Bill's family called from York, as did other friends. It was then that I first realized the vacuum in my life brought on by the loss of my parents a month earlier. Both had died within a few hours of each other, not knowing our plans. I had planned to tell them that summer when they would be visiting us. They never knew my heartaches, but they would have been happy to know that the modest financial bequest they left me was helping realize some of my ambitions, such as owning this home. I am thankful, too, that the virtues they had instilled in me were paying rich dividends.

Throughout the day, we were reminded of our fishbowl existence by the cars passing slowly as their occupants stared or pointed at our house. The volume of traffic increased slowly as the sun began to fade into the west and people started congregating in the streets to the south and east of us. With nothing else to do on a hot summer evening, it was obviously fun to some of them, especially the teenagers, hot-rodders, and motorcyclists. At times the noise was unbearable.

The atmosphere in the neighborhood might have been described as festive except for the five of us to whom it was tragic. It seemed like a real circus atmosphere in many respects. Neighbors hurried in from work to rush through dinner and join the parade. We could see them wave to each other and hear them query, "Hey, going over?" But many people were tense, angry, and upset. They crowded onto the sidewalk and spilled over onto the lawn. Others stood in the streets. Some parked their cars. All eyes were glued to "the house."

Our friends brought us reports from the outside. Rumors sped through the mob. The Quakers had done it...the Jews...the NAACP...the Communists. We were baited, guinea pigs, a test case. "But let's do something," somebody yelled. And then they did—or tried to.

That night about fifty people jammed the small room of the township's municipal building to attend a regular session of the commissioners. Spokesmen protested the police action and asked if the commissioners could do something to get us to leave. "Can't you work out something with this family?" the spokesman asked. "There's no law in this land that says we have to live alongside of them. The family that moved into Dogwood Hollow caused the riot, not us."[5]

The speaker was both right and wrong. He was right that no Levittowner could be legally forced to live beside the Myerses or any other family. It would have been better for us if some of them had exercised their right to move since they did not want us as neighbors. I am certain we would not have made any effort to restrain their liberty to flee.

He was wrong, though, about who caused the riot. That is one of the ironic circumstances of the Negro's attempt to secure for himself the rights and privileges theoretically guaranteed to everyone. He is guilty, in the eyes of the bigot, for seeking that which is morally his. How can the Negro win? He's wrong if he asks and wrong if he accepts the status quo.

The commissioners appeared firm in their reply, expecting their action would nip the ugly protest in the bud. However, a friend of ours who was also a local official told me that the commissioners were just as anxious to see us leave. There was nothing the body could do, the solicitor said forthrightly. "You know as well

---

[5] "Negro Family Insists It Will Move Into Levittown Home Despite Crowds," August 15, 1957, newspaper clipping in author's files.

as I do that the state constitution or federal constitution contains no words that mark out people for black or white."[6]

Leaving the meeting in abject defeat, the mob returned to its more sympathetic setting in Dogwood Hollow. The crowd had grown bigger.

Since the night before, the group I thought of as "the anti-Myerses" had rallied their forces very quickly into the "Levittown Betterment Committee." They had one goal—to force the Myerses out. The leader, James Newell, a southerner who lived a few doors away from us, claimed that the organization would act legally and peacefully. Yet over time he and his cohorts helped create a climate in which violence was almost inevitable.

While the opposition was demonstrating a considerable degree of organization and direction, the forces on our side of the developing controversy were disorganized. Several hundred persons gathered at the William Penn Center seeking a way to help. There was confusion and no leadership available. No one knew what to do, and our reservoir of support was turned away with a promise that they would be called upon later.

The circumstance seems to reflect a characteristic that invariably acts to the disadvantage of progress. The opposition usually organizes first, while the good people's fear or complacency sometimes prevents them from the same sort of display of unity. Those who opposed our move to Levittown had one single purpose—getting us out. Likewise, beforehand they had unanimously agreed that all Negroes should be barred from the community.

Some of the uncertainty among the liberal forces was reflected in the early conversations we held with those who wanted us to move into the house. Though they apparently agreed that a Negro family should move to Levittown, there were differences of opinion about the timing of the move, the best way to ensure its success, the need to prepare the community, and small details that were more divisive than unifying.

Consequently, on our second day at Levittown, we had no organized support on our behalf. We depended upon the small group of friends who stood by us faithfully. The police support continued to be mostly traffic control—moving the crowd back as often as necessary.

Newsmen besieged us, but our friends were our shields and the rioters were the principal source of news. We saw no need to dignify the controversy by engaging in a newspaper debate over a matter that to us was above the level of petty prejudice.

The second day of persistent resistance to our move forced us to think more seriously about the safety of our children. We discussed it with our friends and reluctantly concluded that it would be wise to take them to York until the crisis subsided. Though we hated to see the family divided, we packed the children's clothes before leaving for the night.

The oil tank still was not repaired, and we left a bit earlier than the previous night to return to our Bloomsdale home. The police escorted us nearly all the way.

We initially thought we should take all three children to York, but because Lynda was so young, we decided to keep her with us. I felt that she would be too much of a burden on Bill's family with a formula to prepare and the additional

---

[6] Ibid.

attention an infant requires. I remember saying to Bill that if we were killed in the house, Lynda would be too young to know. At least we would have the boys to carry on. I'd never thought much about immortality, but here I was being forced to examine the meaning of life as well as death. Still, I could not reason why Levittown had to be the stimulant for this involuntary self-examination.

Meanwhile, the crowds still battled the police. Some gathered on the lawn adjacent to our house and talked loudly. "We spent a lot of money on our homes. Now they are worth nothing," one distraught man shouted. Another admitted, "This is why I moved out of Philadelphia." A woman said, "They must be a nice family for whoever persuaded them to move here naturally picked a model Negro family. It's the families that will follow that worry me." One neighbor suggested that we be persuaded to move within thirty days.

About midnight, another stone was thrown by a teenager, but adults restrained him and no damage was done. The skirmishes between the crowds and the police continued late into the night. Two more people were arrested for disorderly conduct: Eva Dombroskie and James Sexton. A newspaper article said that Mrs. Dombroskie "had been running from house to house and shouting to passing motorists in an effort to incite others."[7]

The next morning—Thursday—we left for York, two hours away.

This time York was different. It was no longer the place that had seemed so unfriendly. It was now our haven, our escape from the howling, jeering mobs of Levittown. This was the York we had left, seeking a city that would offer opportunities to all—including those who had been born black. We found peace, but little relaxation from the Levittown situation. Before we could tell the horrible story to our family, local newsmen were on the scene, writing and taking pictures.

I stood there while our photographs were taken and wondered what had happened to the Myers family I knew last week. I felt empty, bewildered, and confused. I closed my eyes and saw the howling mobs, the steady flow of traffic, the prancing police. I was numb and did not hear the reporter say, "Now let's have the Levittown story."

When the house was clear of newsmen and photographers, we repeated the Levittown story to our family, this time more intimately. We talked and talked and, finally exhausted, crept upstairs to bed. But I couldn't sleep immediately. I lay there wondering if our family would be together again soon. How would our boys take the experience of being away from us for the first time? Would we ever reach normalcy again? Would we ever be the same Myers family of just last week?

Our retreat to York avoided a third day of harassment from our bigoted adversaries. Thursday in Levittown was a day of continued mob action, somewhat blunted by effective state police action.

Governor George M. Leader, a native of York County, bitterly attacked the rioters while speaking at a twelve-county meeting in Reading, Pennsylvania. He told the gathering that "the stoning of the home of the first Negro family in Levittown is completely alien to the historic principles on which Pennsylvania was built. . . . Any family has the right to live where it can obtain the right of legal possession—on any street, road or highway in the Commonwealth."[8]

"Mobs Gather at Negro Home," *Delaware Valley Advance*, August 15, 1957.
Philadelphia Inquirer, August 16, 1957, 42.

CHAPTER 5
The First Week in Levittown

At the request of the Bucks County sheriff, C. Leroy Murray, Governor Leader ordered state troopers to guard our home. Sheriff Murray had wired the governor, "Chief of Police Steward of Bristol Township says the citizens of Levittown are out of control. His police…have done all they can to quell the violence in which the Negro's home was stoned and two picture windows broken." Sheriff Murray had also told the governor that the presence of state police would cause the disturbance to be "quelled without bloodshed."[9]

That night—Thursday—the Levittown Betterment Committee probably hit the peak of its popularity with a meeting of more than four hundred held at the John Billington Post 6495, Veterans of Foreign Wars, on Haines Road. James Newell, a past post and county VFW commander, acted as chairman. He insisted that its purpose "was to find a solution to the problem in a peaceful way."

The name they chose for themselves seemed to be a commentary on the twisted logic that can dominate the minds of the prejudiced. A newspaper story had what I thought was the best description of their thinking when the name was chosen. The writer said the decision was made in a "burst of semantic insanity."[10] Friends of ours who attended the meeting said it was boisterous, tense, and inflammatory. There was talk of "blowing them up" and "boycotting all companies" that served us (like that fuel oil company) and "let's go and burn the house down."

Several of the speakers were from outside the area. One identified himself as a Philadelphia tavern owner. All spoke against us and the idea of any Negro family moving to Levittown.

The crowd, angry and tense, left the meeting and headed for our home. They formed a large rectangle and marched two deep in the street, clapping their hands and stamping their feet. There were threats from angry voices and shouts that rose to a crescendo until the police broke up the demonstration.

One person wondered about the people she saw and wrote in a letter to a Philadelphia newspaper:

> Are these the same friendly people who smiled at me on the commuter train this morning? Was that the man who offered me half his newspaper? Are these the kind of neighbors who loaned me their power mower when mine broke down? Are these the considerate people who didn't hesitate to cut your grass and water your tomatoes when you were away on vacation? Are these the same people who sat up half the night with you when your child was sick?

One of the most interesting aspects of those nights came from the later court testimony of Reverend Ray Harwick, pastor of the Church of the Reformation. He and his family had returned from vacation Tuesday, August 13, the day we moved into our new home. On Thursday morning he received a phone call from the president of the Lower Bucks County Council of Churches about the Levittown Betterment Committee meeting scheduled for that evening. Before going to the meeting, Reverend Harwick visited Bill and me to offer us assurance, he said. He arrived at the committee gathering at about 8 p.m. He estimated there were three hundred people gathered on the field outside the VFW.

---

[9] "State Police Guard Home in Levittown," August 16, 1957, newspaper clipping in author's files.
[10] *Bucks County Traveler*, September 1957.

He spotted James Newell. The Bristol Township police also were there. He watched as they stayed outside the crowd and directed traffic.

Reverend Harwick would later testify that he listened as Newell and a few other men stood on a platform and spoke to the crowd. The men had difficulty being heard as people talked and shouted. They prevailed by urging residents to boycott businesses that served our family, such as the Meenan Oil Company. The word *boycott* sent a ripple through some of the people, who urged Newell and the others to avoid using the word as it was illegal to incite a boycott. Instead, they urged the crowd to cancel their contracts with the oil company as a form of protest against serving our family.[11]

Reverend Harwick, one of five clergymen at the gathering, watched the crowd as Newell swore he would do everything within legal and peaceful means to get our family out of Levittown. If those methods failed, Newell vowed, he and his followers would resort to other tactics. In Reverend Harwick's words, "It was an atmosphere of hate… I had never seen hate before, to be perfectly honest about it, and frankly, I was frightened. I didn't know what to expect or what might develop from it."[12]

The Human Relations Council of Bucks County called a meeting that night at the William Penn Center in Fallsington, north of Levittown, to search for ways to give us support. Representatives were present from such groups as Temple Shalom of Levittown, the Fallsington Monthly Meeting of Friends, the Jewish War Veterans, the Women's International League for Peace and Freedom, the Levittown Civic Association, the American Friends Service Committee, and the Levittown Jewish Center.

Another source of public support came from the Bucks County unit of Americans for Democratic Action, which protested the violence and called for full protection by law enforcement agencies. The group's executive committee said, "The right to live where one chooses is a basic American tradition…we believe that there is a place in the community for the Myers family and that they should be treated as any other new residents of Levittown."

The Philadelphia Urban League called on Governor Leader to do everything he could to maintain order in Levittown.

Sympathetic Levittowners tried to get the editor of the local newspaper to editorialize against the violence, panic, and rumor mongering, but he said "no" and left town for a two-week vacation. But a strong editorial appeared on Friday in the *Trenton Evening Times,* titled "Levittown's Shame." It read:

> Levittown, across the river in Bucks County, is a new and attractive community which, so far in its brief history, has a creditable record of good neighborly relations and orderly behavior by its residents. It is in many respects a model town.
>
> The mob attack upon the home of the first Negro family to acquire a home in Levittown is, accordingly, an unfortunate occurrence which has brought the community to ill repute throughout the country.

Commonwealth of Pennsylvania v. Williams et al., September 1957 term.
Ibid.

> This demonstration of racial antagonism reveals an unseemly and repulsive aspect of life in a community whose people enjoy many superior advantages.
>
> Something better in the way of tolerance was to be expected of them.
>
> Instead, several hundred men, women and children gathered at midnight to stone the home of a man and his family of whom they know nothing except their color, which they do not like.
>
> It has been necessary, in view of the spirit prevailing, to seal off a part of the town with police guards to prevent further violent demonstrations.
>
> An admirable and a Christian sentiment has been expressed by the next-door neighbor of the harassed family: "They have a right to live the same as other Americans," he said. "The violence last night was horrible. I hope it ends."
>
> This is the sincere hope of all well-disposed members of the community.
>
> It is not conceivable that this demonstration of mob violence is representative of the spirit of Levittown as a whole.[13]

In fact, the hoodlums did not represent the spirit of Levittown and, at most, there were never more than 600 people in the crowds that gathered. Many of those were teenagers and children. What's more, many of them had only a sight-seer role in the mobs. I'm sure the many sightseers never stopped to think how damaging their presence was. The "anti-Myerses" felt they had their support.

The Betterment Committee kept up its efforts and held another protest meeting Friday night in an open field near the VFW Post because they had been denied the use of any other building. They had planned to meet at the Little League baseball field in the heart of Levittown, but township officials denied them permission.

James Newell continued his irrational and prejudiced harangue through his Betterment Committee. A Negro reporter attended the meeting and quoted Newell as saying among other things, the following:

> Why did Mr. Myers pick our area? Is he a fool or does he think he is better than any other colored person? We will try our best to give Mr. Myers consideration, but are we to allow our happy community to go to pot? Is our community to be destroyed because one individual did not bother to find out whether he is welcome? We must settle by law this situation in which one man did not have the decency and common courtesy to respect the rights of other men.

Meanwhile, responsible elements in the community continued to work diligently to form an organization, and on Friday the newly formed Levittown Citizens Committee had taken shape. It eventually adopted a "Declaration of Conscience," which called for law and order without forthrightly supporting our right to live in Levittown. They declared:

> We, as residents of Levittown, Pennsylvania, stand for the maintenance of law and order.

---

[13] *Trenton Evening Times,* August 21, 1957.

We deplore all acts of violence and intimidation against the Myers family. We are proud of our community and have faith that it will continue to be a good place for all its citizens.

A similar declaration was published the following day in the *Levittown Times* and was signed by the Council of Churches of Lower Bucks County, the Jewish Community Council, the William Penn Center, and the Levittown Civic Association.

Even the VFW took action. The Flemington, New Jersey, VFW post passed a unanimous resolution asking the national commander to investigate whether James Newell, the former post commander of the Bucks County VFW, abused his position in the organization while opposing our move. They called for his expulsion if he was found guilty of unauthorized use of his position.[14]

While we welcomed these evidences of support and would have been pleased to have even more, one cannot resist noticing the absence of direct support for the principle of integration. No responsible leader spoke out for integration and a policy of silence seemed to prevail. The tide might have been turned in our favor had there been a firm commitment. Instead, the silence gave consent to the bigots. A group of ministers met to issue a statement but were unable to agree, and nothing was accomplished. Meanwhile, the press highlighted the violence. The community leadership was silent.

Is it timidity that dictates the declarations that ignore the basic moral principles involved in the Negro's struggle for full equality in housing, or schools, or jobs? Law and order must prevail, but law and order can also maintain the status quo and that's precisely what Negroes are determined to change.

While in York, we stayed in contact with friends in Levittown and knew that tension prevailed. However, the news of the governor's action and the mounting opposition to lawlessness sparked a bit of optimism in us.

In both York and Harrisburg, Bill knew some influential people who were in positions to help. Governor Leader was from York. A former teacher of Bill's in York was now a member of the House of Representatives and a former attorney general had become a judge.

We chose to ask Pennsylvania's attorney general, Thomas McBride, for help. After scheduling an appointment, we drove to Harrisburg to meet with him. When we arrived at his office, we were escorted to a conference room. As the doors were opened, we saw this figure at the far end of the mahogany conference table. The table was quite long—I would think it could fit seventy-five to eighty-five people. As we walked down to meet Attorney General McBride, I saw that he had his feet perched up on the table, crossed at the ankle. I was astonished because Mr. McBride had clubfeet and did not hesitate to let us see that.

This soft-spoken and powerful man welcomed us and said, "I have but one question to ask of you: Do you want to stay in that home?" We said, "Yes." He assured us that we could live there in peace as long as we wanted. "The state police will be there when you return and will remain there as long as necessary." He also said that if peace did not come soon, the state would obtain an injunction against the troublemakers.

"VFW Asked to Investigate Action of Levittown Leader," *New York Post*, August 23, 1957, 41.

Encouraged, we returned Saturday to our Bloomsdale home and attended a meeting of the Levittown Citizens Committee which named Reverend Harwick as chairman. This group gradually took over as the Human Relations Council of Bucks County fell apart.

When the Betterment Committee met again Saturday night, Sheriff Murray told them that no further public meetings could be held. The frustrated mob marched up to Deepgreen Lane and was met by twenty-five state troopers and township police. The crowd was told to keep moving and prodded along by the troopers with nightsticks. One agitator resisted police orders and was charged with disorderly conduct. He was the eighth person to be arrested since the trouble began.

As the black headlines of violence were sensationalized in the nation's press, the crowds continued to stand around nightly. A number of Levittown clergymen returned from their vacations when news of the violence reached them. On Sunday they discussed the situation from their pulpits. Many of them later confessed that few of their congregants supported them in their defense of our right to live in Levittown. One minister was heard saying, "This thing's too hot to handle."

Many churches were in tension. Some experienced deep internal conflicts as to whether they should support us. Others were concerned about what they should do if we requested admission to their churches. One priest said, "We Catholics cannot involve ourselves in activities such as this." From where we stood, it seemed the largest number of agitators were Catholic or their spouses were Catholic.

Human relations in the community was not a major concern of the churches. They claimed that "all men are welcome," but failed to live by the pronouncement. One church in Levittown had carved on its wall in bold words: "Thou art welcome whosoever thou art that enters this church." As far as we could tell, that did not mean the Myers family. One resident told a friend of ours that he was greatly concerned and asked advice from his priest. The story is told that the priest advised him, "Just ignore them."

The Jewish community did not hesitate to take a clear and vigorous position. Although Jews then comprised only about 10 percent of the total population of about seventy thousand (35 percent Catholic; 55 percent Protestant, and 10 percent unaffiliated), every Jewish organization spoke out clearly for our right to be in Levittown. Reverend Harwick, chairman of the Citizens Committee, said, "The best Christians in our town are our Jewish neighbors."

The Jewish Community Council, composed of about sixteen organizations, secular and religious, issued a moving statement which read in part: "Seeing in one man all men, and in one family all families; we welcome to Levittown Mr. & Mrs. William Myers, expecting no more or less than is expected of any member of our community."

The former owner of our house and our friends next door, the Wechslers, were Jewish. This fact was exploited greatly by the anti-Semites of the Betterment Committee who started the rumor that the Jews instigated our move to Levittown.

The same kind of thinking went on in some of the Protestant churches. Our friend Tom Colgan, who favored our move, told us that he visited a church unannounced one night. The church was not far from our home. He discussed our move with the minister, suggesting that Bill and I and our children might decide to attend his church because it was so close. The minister flushed and led the visitor to a group of deacons who were meeting downstairs. The minister explained in front of the deacons that the church was "working with a dozen families nearer to Christ." If the Myerses come in, he said, they would lose those families. One deacon responded that the church might lose these families, but other congregants would become better Christians.

The minister boasted that he had preached for forty minutes the previous Sunday about our right to live where we wanted. He said, "The Myerses can become members if they meet our rules."

Colgan then asked if the church would invite us to worship. The minister replied that although we were free to come to his church, he would not invite us and would not visit us. Colgan suggested we would not visit where we were not welcomed. That must have eased the minds of the minister and deacons. Not all ministers felt this way, but not all ministers lived in Levittown.

After reading a letter from a California minister, we felt strengthened and closer to *him* than we did the minister only a couple of blocks away from our home. He said:

> Dear Mr. Myers,
>
> This is to assure you I am among many who wish for the safety of you and your family. To that end, I have sent the following telegram from our church both to the Chief of Police of Levittown and to the pastor of the First Baptist Church.
>
> We strongly urge you contact all ministers of religion in your city at once and urge them to go to their congregation on Sunday and advise them to exercise a Christian attitude toward the lone defenseless Negro family which has moved among them—the conduct of a few people of ill will is bringing shame on your city in the eyes of the world.
>
> God keep you and strengthen you
> Fraternally,
> J. Raymond Henderson

By the weekend, our oil tank had finally been replaced, and we decided to move to Levittown permanently on Monday, August 19. Our determination was not quite as firm as that might sound, however.

Bill asked me on Sunday, "Daisy, do you think it's safe to sleep there now?"

I said, "Well, we have to make it our first night sooner or later, so we might as well start now."

Chapter 6
Living Under Guard

With our boys still in York, we awoke in our home in Bloomsdale Gardens on Monday, August 19. Bill left early to return to work after a two-week "vacation," if it could be called that, and I gathered up the remainder of our odds and ends of furniture that would be taken to Levittown.

The trip from Bloomsdale to the new home this time was for good. I might have felt some remorse as I left, but there was no room in my mind for such thoughts. I was more concerned with the problems we had already faced and the prospect of further trouble. I felt numb on the outside, but inside I was filled with anxiety and endless apprehensions.

A good friend who lived in Levittown accompanied Lynda and me to our new home. Several other friends were on hand to meet us when we arrived. Four policemen were also there guarding the house.

I climbed out of the car with Lynda in my arms and gazed at the pink ranch house trimmed with white. The house that I thought was beautiful months before now suddenly seemed dull, unattractive, insignificant, and unworthy of all the excitement around it. Instead, the house had a new meaning—it was the "house of doubt."

My steps toward the entrance were steady and accompanied by doubts about the future. Would we be willing to endure the hardships thrust upon us? What would be the extent of ostracism? What of the family's physical welfare? When could we sleep comfortably? Would certain suppliers boycott us? Doubt—doubt that must be dispelled.

I opened the door and saw the hallway blocked with mail—from all over the world, as far away as Australia. I wanted to know immediately what messages the letters bore.

A letter from Oak Ridge, Tennessee, said:

> Stick with it—don't let these prejudiced, ignorant people drive you out of your home. You have as much right to be there as they do . . . an awful lot of people are wishing you well . . . my sister and her husband live in Levittown, and they are among those who think the treatment you are receiving is a disgrace.

A Levittown teacher wrote:

> The world needs more people like yourselves who insist upon the respect that all human beings are entitled to. In time, the small handful of agitators will wither and die. In the meantime, however, please keep your spirits high, for the majority of Levittowners are for you and time is on your side.

Another letter said:

> We have been deeply moved by your troubles. We belong to the so-called white group and, we are ashamed by the behavior of this ugly and hate-infested Levittown Betterment Committee—we hope, however, you will stay in Levittown . . . please stay and fight for what is rightfully yours—the right to live where you please.

CHAPTER 6
Living Under Guard

I was not able to read all the letters immediately, but the few I did read were sufficient encouragement to let me know that we were not alone. Our struggle was just beginning, and now others were helping us make the climb. There were friends in the house, friends next door, friends across the street, friends in many sections of Levittown, and now sympathizers throughout the world. Here was the beginning of one human reaching out to another. These letters were a treasure to us; Bill and I read them with deep satisfaction and cherished each one.

We had been in the house only a short while when we heard a report on the radio that distorted the facts about our arrival. It was presented as a newsflash. The announcer said that Mr. and Mrs. Myers and their daughter, accompanied by several white men, had just moved into their home in Levittown. It also said that Mr. Myers made the statement that "we're here to stay." I suppose the information had been provided by a reporter who had fabricated his story after I declined to talk to newsmen as we arrived.

As the day progressed, we noticed small groups standing around in the streets quietly. As time wore on, they were joined by others and traffic increased.

Bill arrived home from work and was disgusted to see the return of the crowds and newsmen. He was immediately surrounded by questioning reporters. It seemed like an hour before he got into the house, exhausted.

"Oh, Daisy," he said, "I'm ready to give up. Let's call it quits." I suggested that he sit down and read a few of the letters we had received. I was sure they would boost his spirits.

I prepared dinner, but both of us found it difficult to eat. In fact, Bill had to see the doctor several times during the crisis; each time the diagnosis was nervous tension. For a long time, the evening meal was not relaxed; it was not a time we could enjoy. There were always interruptions by reporters and by friends who would drop in with a word of cheer.

We called York daily to talk to the boys and assure our family that we would be all right. But would we?

The job of painting, which we left off the week before, was resumed with the hope that this would get our minds off what was happening or might happen. But no matter what we did, we could hear the grumble of the crowd. We knew they were there—racists, bigots, excitement seekers, curious onlookers, hot-rodders, teenagers, and joy riders. A headline in the paper the day before had read "Tourists Gawk at Negro Home." We had become entertainment for bored people with nothing to do.

With the throng of newsmen pleading for a chance to talk to us, we reluctantly agreed to a press conference. Four friends representing the American Friends Service Committee, the Jewish Labor Committee, and the William Penn Center were with us for the interview. I asked the reporters, "Why don't you newspapermen write about the good things happening to us? One hundred fifty Levittown people have written us letters. Other Levittowners have mowed our lawn, hung our curtains, presented us with a fine oil painting, brought cakes and fruit, and kept us busy receiving well-wishers." Bill told the press, "I intend to stay in Levittown unless there are unforeseen developments. All I want is a chance to be a good neighbor. I bought this house so that my family could have a nice place to live—and all this shouting won't prevent it."

We tried our best to maintain calm in the face of questions—some of which we didn't care to answer. Bill refused at one point in the interview when an adviser tried to get him to quote something from the Bible. We were so sensitive that the suggestion seemed like a stereotype, and what's more, it would be out of character for Bill to quote from the Bible.

He had to try to explain again why we moved to Levittown. He said, "I am a veteran, and I feel that I have a right to live where I choose. I selected my Levittown home because it fits my family's needs." He assured them that we had no outside backing and were strictly on our own.

In the face of the mob action outside, it took courage to express full confidence when asked if we feared the crowds. Bill said, "I'm sure the police will offer protection as long as I need it. I'm certain this will all subside, and the people will go home soon. I know the crowds outside are not indicative of the feeling of most of the people in Levittown. It has been a great strain on us. I hope all this will quiet down, and I'll be able to live a normal life."

A reporter asked if we would consider selling the house at a profit. Our answer was "no." There was not time enough to prepare a formal statement for the press, but it might have been helpful. That would have made it possible for us to state more clearly our motive in moving to Levittown and our determination to stay there. We think it might have made some difference to some people.

We had not minimized the possibility of some kind of incident if we moved to Levittown. We knew that some dark-skinned people already lived there, and we assumed that there was little or no prejudice toward Negro people. Bill had worked in Levittown previously as a service repairman without incident. We were surprised that our move had provoked the kind of demonstrations we were experiencing.

At some point, a question was raised about why we did not choose Concord Park instead of Levittown. Concord Park is the interracial development just north of Philadelphia, which became nationally known as the first project built for open occupancy. We had looked at homes there and liked them. However, Concord Park is farther from Bill's job than Levittown, and it would have taken him longer to get to work. But more than that, the house in Levittown had what we wanted. It was ranch-style and had outdoor space for flowers.

All day I had wondered how Bill was getting along on his first day back at his job. That evening, once we were alone, he told me that most of his colleagues had been nice to him as usual. The union representative had affirmed his support of the move. However, some of the Levittowners on the job had not spoken to him, even though they had been on speaking terms previously.

From six o'clock on that Monday night the crowd increased and got louder and angrier. They booed and jeered during the press conference and were particularly noisy when a newsreel cameraman tried to interview some of the neighbors.

Eventually, the police ordered the growing crowd to move about a block away from the house. They moved reluctantly under the prodding of riot sticks. Some began throwing stones. One hit a state trooper. At that point, the squad commander took to the loudspeaker with an ultimatum: "You have struck one of my men. I will not tolerate this. I give you ten minutes to get back to your homes."[15]

"Levittown, Pa., Mob Jeers 1st Negroes," *Newsday,* August 20, 1957, 4.

Jeers and catcalls answered the ultimatum. The troopers waited patiently for ten minutes while some of the crowd left, but at least half stayed. When the ten-minute deadline arrived, the troop commander announced, "Your time is up." He told his men, "Get them out of here."

Shouts of "Get moving" were mingled with cries of pain as some troopers caught up with those who moved too slowly. Several of the women were struck on the buttocks with riot sticks and, in less than a minute, the street was cleared, although the crowd re-formed about two blocks away. One of the women who was hit was treated at a hospital for shock. Another who spoke English poorly and had been in the United States only a month hollered, "Gestapo! This is America! I came here to be free; now I have to live with Negroes!" Three people were arrested.

A man struck on the head had to be treated for a scalp wound. He is reported to have said later, "I guess I didn't move fast enough." Ironically, this particular Levittowner had been in trouble with his neighbors because of the filthy condition of his property. Neighbors had taken a petition to force him out of another section of the neighborhood, and here he was protesting our move in.

The show of force when the police and state troopers moved the mob back two blocks to Haines Road got results. After joking and singing off their emotions, the crowds drifted away, and our section of Levittown could relax through the few remaining hours until another day dawned. Even Levittown's new Negro residents managed to get some sleep under the encouragement of two friends who remained on guard in the house throughout the night.

Daisy Myers and her infant daughter, Lynda, in Levittown in 1957.

An overview of the area showing Levittown's location and proximity to major eastern cities.

STICKS 'N STONES:
The Myers Family in Levittown

Levittown: "It looked like an ideal place for our growing family."

The first night: "One of the mob had hurled a rock that broke our picture window facing the street on the south side of the house."

"It seemed like a real circus atmosphere in many respects. Neighbors hurried in from work to rush through dinner and join the parade."

STICKS 'N STONES:
The Myers Family in Levittown

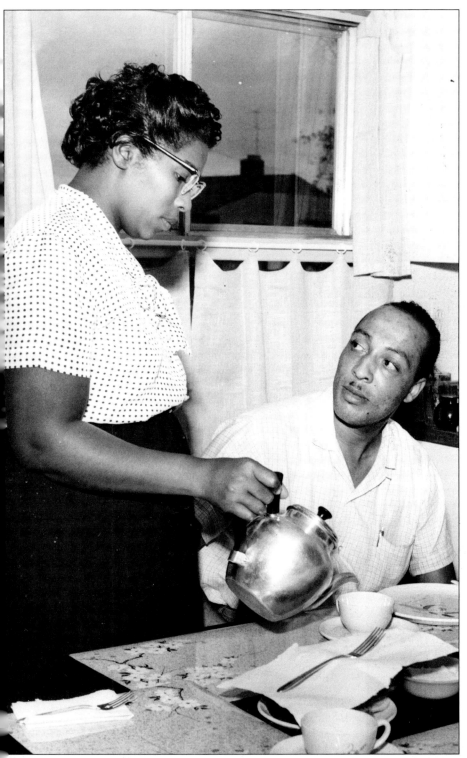

"Despite all that had happened, I hoped we could have a normal day and get some of the chores done. First, there was breakfast to be prepared."

"With the throng of newsmen pleading for a chance to talk to us, we reluctantly agreed to a press conference...Bill told them, 'All I want is a chance to be a good neighbor.'"

"Nightfall always came too soon, for it was then that the crowds began gathering."

STICKS 'N STONES:
The Myers Family in Levittown

"Shouts of 'Get moving' were mingled with cries of pain as some troopers caught up with those who moved too slowly."

"That night...the Levittown Betterment Committee probably hit the peak of its popularity with a meeting of more than 400 held at the John Billington Post 6495, Veterans of Foreign Wars on Haines Road."

"A three-minute deadline was set for the crowd to disperse and go home. Some moved out, but some didn't."

STICKS 'N STONES:
The Myers Family in Levittown

"The crowd was told to keep moving and prodded along by the troopers with nightsticks."

"Our struggle was just beginning and now others were helping us make the climb. There were friends in the house, friends next door, friends across the street, friends in many sections of Levittown—and now sympathizers throughout the world."

"Thus—after two long months—peace finally came to Levittown and the Myerses. It was a pleasant and welcome peace, something we had not known since we left Bloomsdale Gardens."

Chapter 7
The Public Eye

Our first guest Tuesday morning was a reporter, James L. Hicks, of the *Amsterdam News*, a Negro weekly newspaper. He had hoped to catch Bill before he left for work but was too late.

Hicks had also spent the night in Levittown, so the three of us in the Myers family had something in common with him. We had broken the lily-white pattern of Levittown. Somehow the successful night's sleep had boosted my determination. I remember telling him, "We had a good night's rest in our new home, and we intend to stay here."

It was daylight when the reporter arrived, and there was no angry mob. Instead, three state troopers were on guard. One of them told the reporter that he thought we were crazy. He wondered why a man would expose his family to such treatment.

"Look at the house," he said. "Myers is at work. But how about that woman and the children? What if something happens? Who is she going to ask for help? Suppose the house catches fire?"

The newsman answered that he thought the fire department would take care of that. The trooper was not so certain and continued: "But just suppose the guy who drives that fire truck says he can't get the truck started and someone finds that the rotor is missing from the distributor. After all, you know the driver is not supposed to be a mechanic and the truck won't run without a rotor."

During the conversation, the trooper told the reporter that some people in Levittown had threatened to shoot Bill "down on sight." When reminded that he was there to protect us, he explained his role: "We are here to preserve law and order, and we are going to do that. We will protect you and Myers and anyone else, not because you are who you are, but you are citizens and that's our job."

The two friends, Steve and Tom, who had stayed with us through the night, were still present when the reporter arrived. Steve Remsen of the Jewish Labor Committee and Tom Colgan of the American Friends Service Committee represented a committee of Levittown citizens who had volunteered to make certain that we were never in the house alone.

Soon a couple and their teenage daughter arrived to relieve the two men. The woman and her daughter went to work helping me paint, hang curtains, and get the house in order. The man answered the telephone, which rang almost constantly.

A deliveryman arrived from a drugstore, and before I knew it, he had left a package and was gone. One visitor had paid the messenger. I was surprised to get the allergy medicine, which had been ordered the previous evening to send to one of our boys in York. The druggist had told me that his deliveryman would not come through the mob because he lived in Dogwood. We had been doing business with the store for three years while living in Bloomsdale Gardens.

The other part of the story is a complex illustration of how a fearful businessman reacted. The drugstore that finally handled our business was a partnership. The wife of one of the partners had signed one of the Declarations of Conscience. Within minutes after we had received the medicine, the other partner's wife protested the delivery, fearing "it will ruin our business."

The fear in one half of the partnership intensified after the advertisement carrying the Declaration of Conscience. The day after it appeared, copies of the ad were pasted on the store windows when the owners arrived to open the store.

The druggist's wife who signed the declaration began to get annoying telephone calls in which she was called "nigger-lover." But what happened to the other druggist, the fearful one, has never been fully explained. He never set foot again in the store and virtually abandoned it. His partner, however, continued him on the payroll for many weeks. His wife said he had had a nervous breakdown. The frightened druggist sold out to his partner and, later, opened his own store.

Although we were able to get some of the basic services in our new home, we had been unsuccessful in other attempts. We had never had bread or milk deliveries. The bread man stopped by the first day and offered to serve us. We were interested and asked him to stop by the following week. He never returned. We heard that his truck was vandalized the day after his visit.

The milkman never stopped at our house. We had expected to continue with the same company we had used for several years in Bloomsdale. I called them after we moved and asked for service. They told me that they had never served a family with our name. We owed them ten dollars at the time, but they denied that. A friend called for me and asked that we be serviced. A company representative left the phone to check his books. He came back with the same answer—they did not know us. However, he said they would have the salesman stop by. No one ever did. Two years later, we got a bill for the ten dollars we knew we owed the firm.

Later that morning, the plumbers came to finish installing the hot-water heater. It was not the firm that we had originally hired for the job.

We discovered that we were not the only ones having trouble. Before we moved, the family who sold us the house was having problems of its own. The husband had been fired by his father-in-law from his job as a drapery salesman. The reason given was that he had "brought too much unfavorable publicity" to the firm.

The telephone and doorbell were constantly busy. Every so often, we'd hear something or have an experience that helped lighten the burden. Our experience with the oil distributor was one of them.

The first oil company we called gladly agreed to serve us and sent a supply over immediately. The deliveryman lit the burner, but it went out shortly thereafter. The second call brought a serviceman who was accompanied by a company supervisor who assured us that he was glad that we had moved to Levittown. He said his company's policy was to serve any customer. They, too, had felt the wrath of the anti-Myers faction.

The company had already received about thirty cancellations after the truck had been seen at our home, but the supervisor was confident that the disgruntled customers could not find service equal to what his firm offered. He had talked to some of those who canceled and had decided they were "crazy." One of them said that he was canceling his service because his leader told everyone to boycott the firms that served us. Imagine the shock when he was told by the oil-company representative that "their leader" had not canceled. The stunned customer sheepishly asked that he be put back on the list for service. Later, practically all of them reinstated themselves with the firm.

Bill wondered all day about our welfare and called several times asking, "Are you all right, Daisy? Has anything happened?" I only wanted to know how he was doing. Under his seemingly calm voice, I sensed anxiety and fear. Before Bill got to work that morning, someone had painted on the inside walls of the plant, "Get Nigger Myers outta here, outta here, outta here." Thankfully, it was removed quickly, and Bill never saw it.

Bill's supervisors tried to track down the guilty parties, and traps were set to catch the persons responsible. The act was not repeated. Company and union officials assured Bill that his job was secure and that such acts would not be tolerated.

When the day's mail came, I got a needed gift. There were bundles of letters. I read some of them immediately and was moved by the thought that so many people were throwing their moral support behind us. It was needed. Not all the mail was favorable, however. Cranks and bigots wrote also. The first unsigned postal card read, "Do you know what a Molotov is like?"

Telephone calls of all descriptions came. So many of them were downright stupid. A giggling teenage voice said, "We won't marry your sons, they're black." I told myself she would be doing the human race a favor.

At times during the day, I thought I would go mad with the telephone, Lynda crying, telegrams arriving, and friends coming and going. Groceries were brought in and, gifts continued to arrive—flowers from the florist, cakes, cookies, candy, toys for the kids. A lady who lived in the adjoining section, Junewood, called and wanted to know what she could buy the baby. I told her Lynda had about everything, but we could use more diapers. Within two days, four-dozen diapers arrived without a name or address. The note said, "We're glad you're here. Lots of luck and happiness."

Nightfall always came too soon, for it was then that the crowds began gathering. Shortly after five o'clock, the traffic always increased and people could be seen milling around. However, with the ban on crowds in our block, the people were restricted to Haines Road, a thoroughfare about two blocks north of our home. Even from that distance, we could hear the mumble-jumble of the crowds, the jeering, the shouting, and the booing, and finally, the singing of "America." The rhythm, not the words, must have been the attractive feature.

> America, America, God shed his grace on thee,
> And crown thy good with brotherhood
> From sea to shining sea.
> America, America, God mend thy every flaw,
> Confirm thy soul in self-control
> Thy liberty in law.

A little past nine on Tuesday night, the crowd started to charge the police line. A rock about the size of a baseball was thrown from the crowd. It hit Sergeant Thomas Stewart of the Bristol Township Police. He fell to the ground unconscious.

This was the climax. A resident of the community, a law enforcement officer and a thirty-year-old father of four, had been felled by violence by his neighbors.

The local and state police charged the crowd, and within seconds, the crowd disappeared. The injured policeman was taken to the hospital with a concussion. Several arrests followed. A fifteen-year-old boy was seized, but he pleaded that he did not throw the rock. He was released into the custody of his parents.

Shame must have been in the hearts and minds of all the citizens as they hurried for home, shame that an officer paid by their tax money—a man to whom they looked for their own protection—lay sprawled on the ground with blood gushing from his right ear. As the mob scattered, car licenses were checked. Some of the drivers came from Philadelphia; Camden, New Jersey; and Upper Darby, Pennsylvania.

One of the teenagers who was arrested wrote us a letter that we value highly. We believe the writer was sincere in what he said. He wrote:

> This is just a note I am sending along to attempt to clear up a point. Probably you have seen my name, picture and everything else on the radio, TV, and in the newspapers. I was arrested and dragged from my friends' convertible shortly after Sgt. Stewart was hit with the rock. I wanted to let you know that I harbor no malice against you or your family, and I was never once among the mob, which has been creating such a disturbance in Levittown. I was never even out of the car when I was arrested. All I did was count the officers and they were so angry that they thought I said something else and, consequently, came my arrest. I have no objections to you living there, as I am sure most of your neighbors don't object. I hope you can believe this and do not think that I was one of the rioters.

We decided not to see the press during the day. We thought about inviting them in but later decided to issue a prepared statement instead. We had no experience with the media before all this happened, and I'm sure we did not always handle the problem in the best way. In the statement, we tried to express appreciation for the sympathetic understanding shown by the press. We were trying to ask that we be left alone and permitted to live a normal life, if possible in the crisis-like atmosphere.

During that second week, Bill was approached on the job by the Bucks County assistant district attorney who proposed to give us $15,000 for the house. That would have been a $3,000 profit on a house we had stayed in only one night. The man said he represented a few people and that it could be a quiet deal.[16] "It would be best," he said, for all concerned if we accepted the proposition and moved away. The offer was presented in the tone of a mild threat, but Bill said "no" firmly. Several efforts were made to reach Bill on his job and discuss the matter, but Bill refused to talk about it. By this time, the house had taken on a different meaning to us—it was like a fortress with pro-Myers people inside and anti-Myers people outside.

Tuesday's events seemed to mark a turning point. The stoning of the local policeman served as a wake-up call to the community. They realized this could happen in any situation where the forces of law and order are overcome by

---

[16] "Bucks Attorney Offered to Buy Negro's Home," *Philadelphia Evening Bulletin*, n.d., in author's files.

violence. Again, the sheriff banned gatherings and began to take control of the situation. We began to feel that peace might prevail in Levittown. There was other evidence that decent people were beginning to take a stand on behalf of law and order. And some of our supporters began to take a position based on what was morally right. We were encouraged that others were taking a stand to support the right of a citizen to have and enjoy a home he could buy.

A statement from the Catholic Interracial Council of Philadelphia urged "Catholic families to exercise clear judgment and to promote, through prayer and example, a spirit of true Christian neighborliness in their community." The statement said, "The only possible solution for grievous social disorders arising from racial differences lies in the application of Christ's teachings."[17]

Meanwhile, the Levittown Betterment Committee was having trouble finding a place that would allow them to meet. The Committee canceled a meeting set for Wednesday, admitting that its request for use of the Edgley Fire House had been turned down. James Newell, chairman of the group, said that they had decided to try to work through the Levittown Civic Association. He admitted that the latter organization was legally established to represent the people of Levittown.

Newell denounced the stoning of the policeman and said, "I am disgusted with what happened up there last night. It was unjustified and uncalled for. I have always advocated complete cooperation with the police."[18]

The two opposing groups, the Citizens Committee and the Betterment Committee, argued the controversy Wednesday night at a meeting of the Kiwanis Club. The Reverend Ray L. Harwick represented the Citizens Committee, and Newell spoke for the Betterment Committee. Both agreed that they opposed any effort to move us from Levittown by force, but that was all they could agree on.

The local newspaper's account of the Levittown Betterment Committee meeting left us wondering about Reverend Harwick. He reportedly told the group that the Citizens Committee had a neutral stand on integration. He said, "I don't like what has been done to bring the man here," and charged that we had consulted with persons who had given us irresponsible advice. When I later asked him about these statements, he replied that he was misquoted. "Everything was twisted that I said."

James Newell claimed that his opposition to us was not bigotry. He said he was from Durham, North Carolina, and grew up with many close friends who were Negroes. He claimed that it had been proven that property values decline when Negroes move into a neighborhood. However, he did not say who had proved it. He also talked about the large percentage of unwed Negro mothers in Philadelphia but said nothing of unwed white mothers. The statistics he used about property values being lowered were disputed by a speaker at the meeting who said that property values in Levittown, New York, had gone up since about a dozen Negro families moved there. Newell admitted that there was no legal way to force us out but maintained that the Betterment Committee hoped to persuade us to leave.

Reverend Harwick suggested that a joint meeting of the two groups be arranged, but Newell avoided committing himself or his group by saying that he could not find a place to meet. He said there was no place large enough to hold such a meeting indoors. For three hours, the debate went on, but apparently neither side could claim victory.

---

[17]"Police Ban Crowds; Township Officer Hurt," August 21, 1957, newspaper clipping in author's files.
[18]Ibid.

Joseph Segel, the president of the Levittown Civic Association, was reported to have said after the meeting that Reverend Harwick seemed to have a "void in his information about the Negro family moving here." Segel said that his organization heard a report in July that the Human Relations Council was planning to move a Negro family to Levittown. We knew nothing of that at the time and were not involved in any way.

Our situation was pulled into the political arena by a Republican leader who bought an ad to criticize the action of law enforcement officers in trying to control the mob. His ad said:

> I protest the vicious outburst of brutality brought upon the people by the Pennsylvania State Police Troopers in what was described as a peaceful demonstration against the invasion of our community by the Negro. There was no cause Monday evening to beat and kick men, women, and children for no other reason but to dispel hundreds of curious residents, not the riotous mobs described by the State Police Officers. People of this community also deserve consideration and protection being poured upon our Mr. Myers. Mr. Myers—if you are the peace loving homebody your friends make you out to be—then look around you at the violence and disruptions in a once peaceful suburban community caused by your moving here—and go back where you came from.

The same day, the Bucks County YWCA directors ran an ad in which they expressed regret at the reception some residents of Levittown had given us and urged that a "Christian spirit should prevail."

An uneasy peace fell on Levittown—the mobs were off the streets and the traffic was almost normal; the storm had blown over, we surmised. But tension lingered. Residents learned new things about their neighbors. Church members discovered that their ministers preached brotherhood but were not guided by it. Children learned prejudice from their parents. Politicians sat on the fence and spoke positively to positive people and negatively to negative people. The local newspaper carried no editorials about our situation, but two years later in that same paper, I read a half-page editorial on Mack Charles Parker who was lynched in Mississippi.[19]

Underneath the surface, the tension simmered. The chief of police suggested that we had Communist backing and that Reverend Harwick might be a dupe for the Communists. This unnerved Reverend Harwick enough to call for an investigation of us. Of course, we were cleared. At the time, we knew nothing about the investigation. Then he demanded a check on five members of the Citizens Committee. They all protested that Communism was not the issue but rather our right to live in Levittown. Terrified and immobilized, Reverend Harwick did nothing, and the Citizens Committee did nothing as a group. It is amazing how often "Communism" is blamed for our many everyday problems.

Reverend Harwick, who was more or less shoved into the position as chairman of the Citizens Committee because he was a white Christian, had no previous integration ties, nor did he belong to any so-called liberal organizations. The "no

---

[19] *Editor's note:* Mack Charles Parker was charged with raping a white woman in Poplarville, Mississippi. On April 25, 1959, he was taken from his jail cell by a white mob. Two weeks later his body was found in the Pearl River. See http://foia.fbi.gov/parker.htm for the FBI investigation.

Quakers, no Jews" (pro-Myers) people felt this was a very important factor in dealing with this touchy Levittown situation. I disagree with this contention because a man may have all the above-named classifications and still be a failure as a leader. A leader must be genuine, have the cause at heart; he must be fully experienced with the situation and know for what he stands. He must possess the fundamental knowledge necessary. Here was an honest man who said he did not know what civil rights meant. He had never preached a sermon on brotherhood in his years of ministry. Yet he was leading the people along these paths. How could a man with his leadership ability be so unaware of the pressing problems of his day? He said very early in the crisis, "I knew Negroes were out there—somewhere out there—but I was never affected."

It is hard to evaluate Reverend Harwick's actions. He gave the outward impression of meaning well, but his actions were sometimes questionable. A bigot's program is clear at all times—"Keep Negroes out by all means." The well-meaning people under Reverend Harwick's leadership did not have such a clear-cut message. When we needed the Citizens Committee most, it seemed they were too busy arguing among themselves or conducting loyalty checks of innocent people who were only on the Committee to see that our constitutional rights were not denied us.

"You are as clean as whistles," Reverend Harwick stated as he came in our home on one of his very rare visits.

"What are you talking about?" I asked.

"I had you and Bill investigated and, as far back as they could trace, they could find no wrong."

As long as I live, I will never forget those words.

While the Levittown Citizens Committee was frightened into silence over Communism, the bigots were determined to get us out. They knew their goal. It was clear. In that respect, they were in a stronger position than the other groups. They were not concerned about Communism. They were concerned about the Ku Klux Klan and were determined to avoid a precedent by letting us stay.

As the opposition continued, we were blessed by the many deeds of kindness toward us. Many additional Levittowners let us know we were welcome. Our lawn was mowed, more food was brought, and visitors continued to come. A friend I had known previously from the Country Club section, who had a full-time servant, came and scrubbed my floors.

Mail continued to come from all over the world, expressing faith in us and urging us to stick it out.

Some letters read:

> Dear Mr. & Mrs. Myers,
> I'm just one of those "wild" teenagers, seventeen to be exact, but I just have to write to you folks. I was just disgusted with the actions of the people against you. I read all about it in the Star Weekly. I would just like you to know that there's people around here who feel and know that you are equal and should be treated as an equal. At least I'm sure the people of our town must feel that way. I know I do. I just can't understand why they

don't make you their friends! There's good whites, good Negroes and good Indians, just as well as bad whites, bad Negroes and bad Indians. But why do the whites treat the good Negroes bad? This is a stupid letter, but I just had to write to you and send my best of luck to you. Perhaps the crazy people will soon learn some Christian laws and repent. I sure hope so. I am white myself, but if the whites were all like the majority in Levittown, well, I would be ashamed of my colour. Thank you for reading this. If you ever come to Sommerside, P.E.I., you'll find a home at our place.

    Sincerely,
    Miss Gerene Gallant
    Box 114, Summerside, P.E.I., Canada

August 20, 1957
Dear Mr. & Mrs. Myers, Jr.,

I just want to let you know I am very sorry to read of the shocking treatment you have been getting at the hands of vicious, ignorant people. I hope that some way, some how, they will learn to be good neighbors.

    Best wishes,
    Elaine Brown (white)

August 26, 1957
Mr. William Myers
Levittown, Pennsylvania
Dear Mr. Myers:

Congratulations to you and stand continuously for the right. The few who oppose you now are but nothing compared to the millions who are for you.

God's choicest blessings upon you.

    Sincerely,
    Nelson B. Higgins, Jr.
    Minister, Normandie Avenue Methodist
    Church, Los Angeles, California

August 26, 1957
Dear Mr. Myers:

May I just say that, in this whole community, we have been following with a sense of shame the outbreaks which some retarded members of the human race saw fit to organize. We wholeheartedly wish you and your family a happy, quiet life in the home you so well deserve. We also are confident the people of Levittown will come to their senses and make you feel at home. We are sure you are completely right when you said that these demonstrations did not represent the true feelings of the people of Levittown.

    With best wishes,
    Very sincerely yours,
    Konrad Beiber, Ph.D.
    Associate Professor of French,
    Connecticut College, New London, Conn.

Chapter 8
Meetings and More Meetings

By Thursday, August 22—eight days after we had moved—I think we began to relax a bit. A curfew had been set for teenagers, and there was no mob at our house that night.

The Levittown Civic Association held a meeting attended by several hundred to determine, by a poll, if residents of Levittown wanted us to stay in the community. No one ever explained what would be done with the results of the poll, and I never heard if it was conducted. The group also decided to protest the "state police brutality" if persons struck would sign statements that they were hit. The meeting adjourned with the understanding that more could be accomplished with small committee action than by larger groups.

The Levittown Betterment Committee continued agitating the situation and defied the sheriff by announcing that it would continue to hold public meetings. It issued the following statement:

> The Levittown Betterment Committee has not disbanded. In fact, over the weekend, the organization has gained strength and intends to stand upon its constitutional rights and the right to free and peaceful assembly.
>
> We denounce the actions of C. Leroy Murray, sheriff of Bucks County.
>
> We wish to announce openly to Sheriff Murray that we are calling another meeting this week in direct reference to his threat of denying us our constitutional rights.
>
> We want all Levittowners to join us in decrying the only real violence to date: the brutal clubbing of one of the citizens of Levittown by the Pennsylvania State Police.

They found support from other groups. A paid advertisement in the paper from a group identified only as "Quincy Hollow" read:

> To all those supporting the Myers' move to Levittown: Whatever your motives may be, please do not use accusations of violence, prejudice, and discrimination to hide them. . . .
>
> You are discriminating against non-Negroes if you allow Mr. Myers his choice of neighbors but forbid whites from this privilege. . . .
>
> Mr. Newell, we appeal to you to keep us informed of your accomplishments, and advise us on how we can help you. We are eager to cooperate, for we believe you are far more right than a minority of greedy hypocrites.

A source of support came at this point from the United Steelworkers of America. One of its directors issued a statement that said:

> We call upon our many members in the Levittown area not to participate in any un-American acts of bigotry, but to aid and assist in stopping such actions against a family because they happen not to be white.
>
> The desire for a better home and a better way of life is truly American and the right of every American to seek to better himself and his family is a fundamental principle of our union.

CHAPTER 8
Meetings and More Meetings

This veteran, William Myers, Jr., and his family have an inherent right to a better home, a right he has fought to protect, and a home he has worked and saved to buy and, as an American citizen, he and his family are entitled to the full protection of the law.

The local newspapers appeared with two hundred names and addresses of Levittowners who used an ad to publicly let it be known that we were welcome. The following day, another two hundred names appeared. Eventually, more than six thousand names were secured. Both ads carried an open letter to citizens of the community signed by Reverend Harwick in his role as chairman of the Citizens Committee. He wrote:

> I feel certain that you, along with the overwhelming majority of Levittowners, have been shamed and saddened by the violence which has soiled our community. The rock-throwers and the agitators are not representative of the people of Levittown. Undoubtedly, you have wished for some way to express your own conscience and faith in your community. You now have that opportunity. Hundreds of your neighbors have already signed the declaration which appears below. A neighbor will call on you soon. I trust that you will join with all who wish to stand up and be counted for religious morality and decency in our community.

The committee had adopted its Declaration of Conscience a few days earlier.

The same day other organizations announced their support in statements to the press. The Friends Service Association and the Women's International League for Peace and Freedom both spoke out against those who were trying to get us to move.

The Friends Service Association, which operates the William Penn Center in Fallsington, held a special meeting of its board of directors to take action. The association's statement said,

> The Friends Service Association, in accordance with the American democratic ideal and the Quaker principles of long standing, feels that each individual is entitled to fair and equal treatment before the law by his neighbors.
>
> We believe the time is here when an American family of any creed, color, or national origin should be welcomed as new residents.
>
> Where a family meets unfriendliness because of differences of color, creed, or national origin, it violates our highest religious, moral, and political principles as citizens in a land of traditional constitutional liberty.

The association also decided to place its full staff at the disposal of groups in Levittown working on our behalf. The organization felt a need to encourage discussion of both sides of the issue and extended an invitation to use the William Penn Center as a meeting place.

It was the Bucks County chapter of the Women's International League for Peace and Freedom that first openly declared itself in favor of integration. While all the statements by various other groups were welcome, we thought this one was somewhat more courageous than the others, which had managed to skirt the crucial issue. For us, the fundamental question was our basic right to live there, as Pennsylvania Governor George M. Leader and many others had said.

The league's statement read:

> Basic to our democracy is the fundamental truth "that all men are created equal, endowed by their Creator with certain unalienable rights, that among these are life, liberty, and the pursuit of happiness."
>
> Unless these principles are put into practice in community patterns of living, they have little worth.
>
> We are grateful that many of the people of Levittown are speaking out with expressions of good will and tolerance in a truly democratic spirit. We are grateful, too, for the feeling that seems to predominate, to keep the issue on a nonviolent basis.

The executive committee of the Bucks County Chapter of Americans for Democratic Action had taken action on August 14, the day following our move, but it was made public August 22. It protested the mob violence and concluded, "We believe that there is a place in the community for the Myers family and that they should be treated as any other new residents of Levittown."

With the publication of a statement from Jewish groups on August 23, we began to feel that support for us was cutting across many lines. This statement was unanimously adopted by the Levittown Chapter, Women's Division of the American Jewish Congress and the Bucks County chapter of the American Jewish Congress. It, too, deplored the action of bigots and stated:

> [The Congress is] unequivocally committed to the preservation and extension of the democratic way of life. The Congress is dedicated in its program to eliminate all forms of racial and religious discrimination. Only by assuring to all Americans the rights of life, liberty, and property as guaranteed by the Bill of Rights can we gain for ourselves and our country peace, security, and equality of opportunity.

One rather bitter and sarcastic editorial attack was made against the mob violence and opposition groups and said that Levittown was disgraced. I liked these particular lines from the editorial:

> They don't want him [Myers] and his family, and the question is, why not? Because these homes are such frail mansions that the presence of members of another race may jar them? Because, having eagerly bought their mass homes for convenience, the folks are upset because the mass is, after all, really with them? Because it may quite possibly turn out that the Negro family will eventually make a richer contribution to national life than one or two of its white neighbors?[20]

---
[20] *Delaware Valley News* (Yardley, Pa.), August 22, 1957.

Some folks in the first Levittown, on Long Island, wanted us to know they were sympathetic. That Levittown, like this one in Pennsylvania, and the third one in New Jersey, began as all-white communities. Negroes finally moved to Levittown, Long Island, after years of effort. Their citizens went all out for us, showing support with many letters, gifts, visitors, and the like. There were many other invitations to come and visit, bring the family, stay as long as we wished, and get away from the unpleasantness here in Levittown.

A post of Jewish War Veterans in the Long Island Levittown accused the Betterment Committee of casting "a great blot of shame and degradation" on the name of Levittown. The Levittown, Long Island, Regular Democratic Club praised Governor Leader for backing us. In a letter to the governor, the club president said, "We have been greatly heartened by your clear-sighted and uncompromising statements."

Other political figures spoke publicly about Levittown, too. Richardson Dilworth, Philadelphia's mayor, addressed over five thousand members of the Imperial Council of Shriners at Convention Hall. He said, "I know that the southern advocates of segregation must be sitting back getting a horse laugh out of what is happening in Levittown."[21]

The news stories made little or no reference to the good—what appeared in print was all bad. Five hundred persons were reported on the corners, but no mention was made of the thousands who were asleep in Levittown homes. Food, flowers, money, and gifts were not mentioned as a rule. The only thought clearly conveyed was "to get the Myerses out of Levittown." A good example can be found in the Philadelphia *Sunday Bulletin* of December 14, 1958. Newsmen and photographers flocked to Clinton, Tennessee, when a school was blown up. It hit the front pages all over the country. A bombed-out building is always news, but when something good happens—like a new school being built—it is not news because it does not make for dramatic, gruesome pictures. However, the manner in which ordinary people all over the nation chipped in to help rebuild a schoolhouse is, nevertheless, one of the biggest stories in the nation.

The Levittown-Myers excitement spilled over into Philadelphia on August 23 when the Betterment Committee crowd appeared on Frank Ford's midnight show on radio station WPEN. Some fifty policemen were sent into the area hours before the broadcast. All sorts of rumors spread throughout the neighborhood. No one knew why the police were on hand. The general belief was that wherever the Betterment group appeared, there always resulted great confusion and disorder.

The notice in the newspaper about the radio meeting quoted Betterment Committee member John Piechowski: "This is the general meeting we promised to hold for our group.... We are inviting all Levittowners, who feel the way we do, because this is our meeting." The room held two hundred people, but Piechowski made it clear that they didn't welcome everyone. "Since this is our meeting, we want only those who agree with us to call in."[22]

For three hours, the spokesmen of the organized haters talked anti-Myers. It was more of a comic sideshow and was enjoyed even by those who were on our side. Frank Ford, who conducted the show, deserves praise for the patience he

---

[21] "Dixie Likes Levittown," *Pittsburgh Courier*, August 31, 1957.
[22] "Betterment Group Sets Radio Meeting," *Levittown Times*, August 23, 1957.

showed amid the ignorance of James Newell and his followers. For all the talking they did, what they said could be boiled down to the simple fact that they did not want an American Negro family in Levittown—period.

The Betterment Committee folks hurt their cause by the public broadcast of their arguments. It was obvious to thousands who listened that here was a group of rabid bigots, unable to reason, think, or express themselves intelligently. If they won any sympathy by the broadcast, it probably was more because of their stupidity. Even those who disagreed could be charitable with characters of their kind.

We continued to experience a period of quiet while rumors flew about us. Most were silly and could be ignored. One such rumor was that we used silver ashtrays for our guests (in reality, tinfoil potpie pans). A more serious rumor, however, was that a Negro family was planning to move into the North Park section of Levittown. That house was vandalized with several hundred dollars worth of damage because of this rumor.

Another incident of terror spread to a family in a section of Levittown about five miles away from us. They were accused of selling to Negroes simply because they interviewed a Negro for a job. Months later in court, the homeowner was asked about his experiences. He said, "It was in September. Two men came to my house about six-thirty or seven o'clock at night and told me that they had heard colored people were either moving in or had moved into our home. . . . I became annoyed, and then after a while, I explained that this wasn't true and, in the meantime, there were cars coming by." He was asked by the court to explain what wasn't true, and he said, "That we had sold our house to colored people, or colored people had moved into our house. . . . [After I answered their questions] these two men went out and told the people who were coming by that it wasn't true and that was the end of it."[23]

When the mob action had been silenced, police finally left their daily guard of our house. We felt that life was beginning to take on a normal pattern. Our friends and supporters were optimistic. We began moving about freely. Friends stopped in often, and the mail continued to arrive in large bundles. Our morale was high, but we still felt the need for maximum community support. We were aware, however, of the silence of individuals and organizations that had made one big public stand and apparently withdrawn from the fray.

We appreciated those who stood firm in their efforts to support and encourage us, but too many others had adopted a neutral pose in a situation where there could or should not be neutrality. Some individuals gave me the impression that they meant well and were willing to do almost anything for us as long as it cost them little or as long as the task was convenient and would not hurt them. Some expressed their greetings to us via letter or telephone. People would say they would like to see us but did not feel they could drop by *"just yet."*

Bill and I wondered what might happen next—if anything. It was a relief to have the tension eased, but somehow, we could not be sure. Subsequent events justified our caution about the future.

---

[23] *Commonwealth of Pennsylvania* v. Williams et al., September 1957 term.

Chapter 9
Little Rock Comes to Levittown

It had now been eight days since the moving van pulled up to our front door. For the next several days—the week before Labor Day—we experienced our first taste of normal life in Levittown. But still it was not really *normal*. While the community seemed quiet on the outside, the tension continued. Fear contaminated our inner lives and immobilized our sympathizers. It was much like sitting on a keg of gunpowder—would it explode or not? The air swirled with rumors. An active member of the Betterment Committee was reported to have made a trip to get dynamite. Another rumor said a mass picket was scheduled for eight o'clock one evening, but a few minutes before eight a pouring rain washed away that possibility. I have no doubt that the picket was planned, but I also do not doubt the hand of God in the rainstorm.

The state police were no longer guarding our house, but our friends stayed on as guards, just in case. We were tempted to think that our antagonists had seen the futility of their bigotry, but some incidents showed such thinking would be in error. Our guards gave the state police the license numbers of about thirty suspicious automobiles. One night—about three in the morning—a man stopped and asked why the Myerses were being protected. The guard replied that he was trying to help his friends. In the exchange, the rude character argued that the police could take care of the situation. True, the local police could have, but they never did, and that is probably the most important element in our story. Local law enforcement was most ineffective.

Despite the rumors and the continuing parade of cars driving by the house, by comparison with what we had just experienced, now was a period of calm. I'll always feel that we might have moved on from that point to a gradual reconciliation since there was positive evidence that the opposition had been broken. This was a reasonable assumption at the time, but we had not anticipated the actions of Governor Faubus. We had never even heard of this man, but his actions were about to make things worse.

On September 2, Arkansas Governor Orval Faubus ordered the state's National Guard to surround Central High School in Little Rock to prevent nine Negro students from attending classes and integrating the high school. The next day Federal Judge Ronald N. Davies directed the Little Rock school board to disregard the troops and permit the nine students to enter the school. However, on Wednesday, the National Guard and state troopers, under orders from Faubus, would not allow the Negro students to enter the school.[24]

Had Governor Faubus been reading about our story during the past two weeks? No doubt he had. I've often wondered what he might have thought about integration in Levittown as he faced the possibility of school integration in Little Rock. Of one thing I am clear: The two events, though many miles apart, had an impact on each other. We saw the evidence first-hand.

We immediately began receiving clippings from unidentified correspondents. The message was obvious. Each article seemed to emphasize how the law could successfully be disregarded. After all, Governor Faubus had defied the U.S. Supreme Court and a federal judge. We received telephone calls praising

---

[24] *Editor's note:* The standoff in Little Rock would last for weeks. The National Guard was finally withdrawn on September 20 and the students entered Central High School for the first time under heavy police protection on Monday, September 23, with support from President Dwight Eisenhower coming a day later. On Wednesday, September 25, the 101st Airborne escorted the students, who would become known as "the Little Rock Nine." See www.centralhigh57.org for details.

Governor Faubus. He was "the type of man we needed in Levittown," they said. In fact, we had his "type" already, and we held them all in contempt.

Bigotry in Levittown bound us emotionally to those nine Negro students. We watched the sordid Little Rock story on television and read the newspapers. We wondered how the events in Levittown and Arkansas would influence each other.

We did not have to wait for long. Friday morning, September 6, our "uneasy calm" was broken. While I was preparing breakfast, a strange odor attracted my attention. I knew it couldn't be the food on my stove, but somewhere in my memory I thought I should be able to identify the smell. I looked out of the window and told myself that something was burning: Could it be wood?

The early morning was foggy and overcast. I could see nothing unusual outside, but the odor persisted and grew stronger as I inhaled. I called Bill and told him to see if the house was afire. He jumped up, threw on his robe, and searched the house inside and out but found nothing.

"Maybe someone's burning trash, but it smells like wood," I said, and went ahead with breakfast.

The telephone rang. It was Lewis Wechsler, our next-door neighbor. When he went out to get his morning newspaper, he had found a five-foot cross burning on his lawn. He called the police first and then us.

I hung up the phone in despair. Now what? How much can we take? The quiet period was over. This was the start of something new—we knew not what.

We wondered if it was time to give up and forget Levittown. It was obvious that the intimidation and harassment would continue. We could not depend on the local police—then or ever. Levittown clearly had a rabid army of bigots who preferred wallowing in their prejudices.

The Wechslers were friends of ours before we moved to Levittown. They were members of the William Penn Center group and had publicly defended our right to own a home anywhere we chose. The day we first moved in, Lewis Wechsler went outside and tried to convince the protesters to leave. One neighbor asked him if he was a "nigger lover." Another neighbor, Barney Bell, suggested Lewis go back into his house before the crowd turned on him. The Wechslers were to pay dearly for speaking up for us.

Although Lewis Wechsler tried to console himself with the belief that the cross burning was a children's prank, it was not the first cross burning in Levittown that summer. Five cross burnings had occurred at three separate schoolyards in August. There also had been a rash of brush fires in the woods near our home.

The cross was attached by wire to an oil-tank vent protruding from his lawn. The young saplings used to make it probably came from the nearby woods. It was crude and bound together with rags that had been soaked with kerosene or gasoline. A jar that might have contained the inflammable liquid was found smashed in the Wechslers' driveway.

The cross wasn't the first incident that week. A few days before, police had found four milk bottles filled with gasoline and stoppered with rags in the shrubbery behind several neighbors' houses. In that case, Police Chief John Stewart told the newspaper that the milk-bottle bombs had nothing to do with the attacks on our house. He said, "We found a similar bottle some time ago after a woods fire in that section." During the past spring, the area had been plagued with small fires in the woods.[25]

Within a few minutes after the cross was discovered, a reporter from a Philadelphia newspaper arrived. Someone called him saying he would find a cross burning on the lawn at our neighbors' address. He claimed he could not identify the caller but said it was a man.

As morning wore on, I noticed many of the bigots of the Betterment Committee driving past and looking. I am sure they wanted to see the results of their dirty work. One of the racists, who was always in the forefront of the demonstrations, came by minutes after the police arrived. He slowed down, took a good look, and sped off. I wondered how he and the reporter had gotten their information about the cross so quickly.

Twilight that evening brought a small group of antagonists out again for the first time since the crisis had eased. They gathered on the corner. Suddenly everybody had a letter to mail. They raised and lowered the letter slot repeatedly with a clang, banging as loud as they could. It was a nerve-wracking noise. Policemen tried to stop them, but they'd say, "All I'm doing is mailing a letter." Giggling women waved and yelled at passing motorists. The men stood around smoking and talking—and, I suppose, planning. As our white friends entered and left, they were subjected to yelling and insulting epithets. As two of our visitors left, a group stood in front of their car and dared the driver to run over them.

Our mail and telephone threats that included derogatory terms indicated that the Ku Klux Klan had entered the picture. In court months later, Sgt. Adrian McCarr of the Pennsylvania State Police testified that our assumptions were accurate. He said he had found literature from the Klan's imperial wizard in Howard Bentcliffe's possession.[26]

Friends and organizations offered to pay for the damages done to the Wechslers' home. They received many anonymous donations. Instead of becoming more fearful, our supporters felt stronger and stronger, really getting angry for the first time.

But the "antis" became more active as well. Some of them rented a vacant house adjacent to ours and formed their own little "club." This latest development caught the attention of *Time* magazine:

> In the rubber-stamp ranch-house community of Levittown, Pa. (pop. 60,000), the vacant house at 30 Darkleaf Lane last week came alive with a distinction all its own. From one roof peak flew an American flag, and from another—spotlighted by night—the stars and bars of the Confederacy. Each evening the house of the Confederacy was crowded with the members of the newly formed Dogwood Hollow Social Club who worked hard at a hard-boiled bad-neighbor policy.[27]

The people who came to that house occupied themselves by making as much noise as they could, whether it was by singing, yelling, clapping, playing records of "Dixie," "Old Black Joe," and "Old Man River" at top volume, or blowing a bugle. Township officials said the gatherings were a violation of the zoning

---

[25] "Fiery Cross, Gas-filled Bottles Found Near Myers' Levitt Home," *Delaware Valley Advance*, September 12, 1957.
[26] "Policeman Reveals Plan for Levittown Ku Klux Klan," December 10, 1957, newspaper clipping in author's files.
[27] "War of Nerves," *Time*, October 7, 1957, 29.

ordinance but took no action right away. A number of people visited the house—newspaper reports estimated fifty to one hundred people—the most notorious being our infamous mailman who had been shocked to face me the day we moved in. While all this was going on, someone managed to sneak over to the Wechslers' and paint a big "KKK" on the side of the house and hang a threatening poster next to it.

Some neighbors complained about the noise even though they may have been sympathetic to getting us out. Other neighbors living near that house did not frequent it but never complained about the noise. Yet when the Wechslers placed a light in the rear of their home for protection, those same neighbors complained to the police that the light was too bright.

I suppose we might have been able to adjust ourselves to the noise campaign, but I'm thankful that it was not necessary. After about a week, William Hughes, the owner of the house, was arrested for violating township zoning ordinances. He was ordered to evict the occupants or face a fine and possibly time in jail. After his hearing, he went back to the house and told the people to leave. The paper quoted him as saying, "This is the only way to keep me from going to jail."[28]

The Betterment crowd cried persecution. They pleaded for the house under pretense that it was being used as a private club, but the law does not permit such a facility in a residential neighborhood. Eldred Williams stayed around after the eviction, supposedly as a caretaker, brazenly going in and out all day and night. He continued some of the club's activities, at times playing the record player at top volume.[29]

We couldn't help but wonder if it would have taken a week to move us out if we had been responsible for the kind of things that happened in that house. We had heard how the township manager, who lived just a stone's throw from us, had broken up a boisterous party in the same neighborhood before we moved to Dogwood Hollow. Now he found it difficult to use the same authority he had exercised without hesitation before Negroes had moved to Levittown.

Though the bigots were ousted from the house, small groups gathered nightly on various "anti" lawns, continuing to sing, jeer, and clap their hands. As the township defaulted on law enforcement, we were forced into a detective role and had to seek the aid of concerned citizens to help protect us and our families. As a result, I acquired a kind of sixth sense, which helped me detect their movements. I learned to know the sound of an automobile that belonged to one of the key Betterment leaders. The silhouette of certain characters seen in the dark was enough to identify them. We had to be—and were—constantly on the alert.

Our experience in Levittown sharpened our sense of sensitivity to possible intimidation and discrimination. Of course, as for any other members of minority groups, this was inherent in our background. I recall how I evaluated a delegation that came to our house to investigate us for the Levittown Civic Association. Since that organization had not been able to do anything positive, I suppose they thought that a fact-finding job might serve some purpose. We doubted it, but agreed to receive the visitors since it might dispel some of the rumors. We have often wondered if anyone investigated or even thought of investigating the first

---

[28] "Gatherings Halted in House Next to Negro's in Levittown," September 27, 1957, newspaper clipping in author's files.
[29] "Myers Neighbor's Home Is Crayoned," undated newspaper clipping in author's files.

Puerto Rican, Indian, Polish, Jewish, Hungarian, or Italian families because they found Levittown a desirable community in which to live.

In their own minds, the delegation undoubtedly felt that they were engaged in a serious undertaking and acted accordingly. Some of the questions had five or six sub questions. I've never been convinced that anything was gained through the experience.

The questions ranged far and wide and pried unnecessarily into our private lives. They also asked questions to which they knew the answers, such as "Do you own this house?" and "Do you own the blue and white 1957 Mercury that is frequently parked in front of this house?"

They asked about membership in organizations advocating integration. They questioned our education, work experience, and our social aims as related to our neighbors. They asked us why we moved to Levittown, why we left Bloomsdale Gardens, if we had any sponsors, why we refused the $5,000 profit for the house, who we thought opposed our move to Levittown.

Question number 13 on our list had been left blank. This question undoubtedly referred to intermarriage. Although it was not on the list, however, they still asked. I carefully explained that Negro parents are just as concerned—or more so—whom their children will marry. No parents move into a neighborhood looking for a mate for their son and daughter.

The questionnaire also included the following:

> Would you encourage or are you now encouraging additional Negroes to move into Levittown? Do you know of anyone who is?
> Do you know of any master plan to integrate Levittown?
> Have you given any thought to moving back to a Negro community because of local pressures?
> Do you think your race has benefited by your move into Levittown and the resulting publicity?
> Have you made previous moves in which you were: the first colored worker at your place of employment; the first colored resident of a community?

What inherent right did they have to ask us these questions? Simply because we moved to Levittown—white Levittown?

Somebody wanted to know if a poll of residents showed we were not wanted, would we move. Our answer was "No."

There were about three decent people in the delegation. One of them was apologetic about some of the questions and tried to soften their impact.

One of the most interesting aspects of the experience was the evaluation of handshakes as they arrived. The decent ones shook hands firmly. The bigots offered a light, "feathery" hand.

Apparently the delegation satisfied itself by the inquiry. It turned out that their main objective was to determine if we were sponsored by an organized group. They told the Levittown Civic Association at its next meeting that we were not sponsored and that there was no knowledge of any other Negroes coming to Levittown.[30] I suppose that gave them some relief—temporarily.

---

[30] "Probers Find No Indication of Myers' Sponsor," October 16, 1957, newspaper clipping in author's files.

Chapter 10
Peace Finally Comes Home

After almost two months of living with the township officials' "wait and see" attitude, we felt their claim that they intended to make our stay in Levittown safe seemed to be almost a joke. Who could believe such pious words in the face of threats and harassment?

Time and again we were advised to seek an injunction against the troublemakers. I remember Barry Gray suggesting it when I was on his radio program in New York. Bill and I were receptive to the idea since we wanted something done to solve the problem. However, we did not want to do anything to increase the personal antagonism against us. We also had to consider the fact that legal action would be expensive. We did not want to increase our financial burden. We kept telling ourselves that if the other neighbors could bear the disturbances, so could we. We suffered, but they suffered along with us, sometimes for the smallest thing. A neighbor stopped to chat with us one evening. When she got home, she found a sign on her lawn that said "nigger lover."

Several highly respected organizations offered us legal aid and assistance. Those closely associated with us felt that it would be more desirable if the state took the necessary action. In that way, the full power of the commonwealth of Pennsylvania would be thrown behind the move for justice and equality. Attorney General McBride was hesitant to enter the case, hoping that the local police would assert their authority.[31] It became apparent, though, that the local police did not want to act and had no orders to act from the board of commissioners. Bill and I felt that we had not caused the trouble, and it was past time for firm action to be taken. There seemed no need to pussyfoot with the pack of jackals and bigots.

Our little cottage at Deepgreen Lane had undergone about all the painting, wallpapering, and general cleanup we had planned, but it was not yet "home." There was little time to enjoy it. By day, I was constantly busy with guests, the new baby, and the two active boys. Fortunately, they were too young to question why they were being kept so close to the house. They had a stern warning against playing in the street where traffic was not yet at a normal pace.

Residents and visitors continued to drive slowly by and stare. They turned around at the corner and stared again in passing as if some revolutionary change had taken place in the few moments between trips. Some of those who came knew only that we lived at Deepgreen and Daffodil Lanes and probably expected the Myers house to be "different" and easy to identify from the four at the intersection. They would point first at one house and then another without knowing which one we actually lived in. Some stopped and asked whomever they saw.

One carload of curious persons was shocked at the answer they received. They told a neighbor that they had heard that Negroes had moved into the block and had come to see what the place looked like. Our neighbor replied that she thought it was nice that Negroes had moved in. "Nice?" said one of the inquirers. "You must be nuts." With that, they sped away.

Our state police guard continued on duty. We kept longing for the day when that would no longer be necessary, but Mr. McBride had assured us that we'd have the protection as long as it was needed.

A partial explanation of the passiveness of local police officials lies in the nature of Levittown. Though it was a community of more than 70,000 persons, it had no

---

"Township Failed to Protect Myers, McBride Charges," *Philadelphia Evening Bulletin*, October 8, 1957.

central municipal structure. There was no central point of leadership. Levittown sprawled over five municipalities. In the eyes of the world, the controversy involved the entire Levittown community, but only a portion of that vast artificial town could assume any legal responsibility for solving our problem. We were part of Bristol Township, and its law enforcement machinery had sole responsibility for law and order.

One event that broke into the papers during the weeks of difficulty indicated that something was wrong in the township police department. The Bristol commissioners awarded a citation to a Bristol Township sergeant for his work in the crisis surrounding our move to Levittown. The officer returned the citation to the police chief with the explanation that he could not accept it "in good conscience." His letter said, in part:

> My personal feeling in the matter is that I was not permitted to enforce the laws as they are written. I only acted as a traffic cop at the scene. Whether or not I agree with what was going on is not the question. I felt it was my job to maintain law and order and to protect the rights and safety of those living or passing through our community, regardless of what they might be. I was not permitted to do my duty as my conscience dictated. I was ordered by my immediate superior not to take action. This was, to me, ignoring my responsibility. Although the board acted in good faith when it awarded the citation, I cannot accept it in good conscience. Therefore, I am taking a dignified step toward improving the department by returning it [the citation] to your charge.

The chief denied the charge, and subsequently, the sergeant was demoted to patrolman. The public announcement said that the action was taken for violation of the township's regulation forbidding the release of information to the press without proper authorization.

The officer's letter came on the heels of a letter from Mr. McBride explaining why he assigned state police to guard our home. Township Manager Rolfe said he did not consider either Mr. McBride's or the officer's letter as "valid."

That was the price an honest township officer had to pay for his conviction. It was an odd consolation to us that here was another victim of Levittown bigotry. But why should any of us have to suffer? It was a troublesome question and one that never should have developed. To put it simply, I believe if arrests had been made at the outset, there would have been no trouble. Even after the difficulties snowballed, wholesale arrests by local police would have curbed the mobs.

We never received widespread community support from the silent sympathizers whose influence could have spurred the law enforcement officers. Their default gave the impression that the masses of Levittowners were behind the actions of the Betterment group. Where were the religious leaders of different faiths and civic and political leaders whose positive action and support could have averted the community's black eye? Even now, the answer could help explain what happened to us and Levittown.

Unanswered questions and disappointments seem to be inherent in the problems of race relations. Both white and black Americans make mistakes, and both groups pass the buck to the other in self-defense.

We had spent a lot of money preparing for the move, as we felt the obligation to make a good impression. Some of the old furniture was not quite what we wanted to take into the new home—particularly since we were Negroes. If we had moved to an integrated neighborhood, I'm sure the furniture would have been adequate. A month before the move, we had bought a new car to replace the seven-year-old one we'd been using. We have noticed whites moving into Levittown who have kept newspapers and sheets at the windows for many weeks until they got around to hanging curtains—this we could not have done.

Like other Negroes, we wanted to avoid strengthening the stereotype of the race. We found it bares its ugly face in some surprising places. Some of our visitors in Levittown were surprised that we did not maintain a well-stocked bar or gamble. It was assumed that I was an excellent cook, though I'd never cooked before I married. Some folks expected Bill and me to be able to sing well. They were disappointed that we could not sing spirituals or quote the Bible to a newsman. Some white liberals seem to place a ceiling on Negro freedom of expression. I got involved in a verbal clash with a builder when I argued against a quota system in planned interracial housing projects. I contended that Negroes do not want a quota or any plan except that available to all other Americans. It's the opportunity to look, choose, and buy freely whenever he sees what meets his need. The Negro does not look for a house because white people live in the community. He wants to drive down a street and pick what interests him, then pursue his interest to the point of ownership.

Sometimes these views cause friction and controversy even among Negroes. The Myers family may be criticized for desertion by moving to Levittown. The critics are missing the point—freedom is basic to the American way of life. They are also ignoring the contributions one can make when any barrier is broken.

The Negro home seeker looks for a place to live with criteria similar to those used by other Americans. He wants, within the possibilities of his ability to pay, the facilities that will provide comfort and convenience as well as intangibles. He seeks neighbors with common interests. He may want a community with a stimulating atmosphere for himself and his children, but what seems to meet his need is denied.

In buying in Levittown, Bill and I thought we had achieved almost the perfect situation. Obviously, we were mistaken—we failed to anticipate the Betterment group.

Finally, on October 18, the impasse was broken. Howard Bentcliffe was arrested for malicious mischief for painting "KKK" on the side of the Wechslers' house and placing the Klan poster next to it, "which featured [a] white woman cringing before a huge Negro . . . [with] the crayoned inscription, 'We are watching your every move.'"[32] In later court testimony, he said he drew lots with four other unidentified men to do the job. He also said that another man drew a lot to burn a cross on the lawn of an auto salesman who was supposed to have sold us our automobile. We had never met the salesman's family, with the exception of their thirteen-year-old daughter, who was one of two teenagers who came with flowers to welcome us to the neighborhood. The salesman was harassed simply because he worked for a Lincoln-Mercury company, and our new car was a Mercury.

---

[32] "Myers Neighbor's Home Is Crayoned," *Bucks County Courier*, n.d., in author's files.

CHAPTER 10
Peace Finally Comes Home

This was not Bentcliffe's first arrest. He and his wife, Agnes, had been among those arrested (on charges of disorderly conduct) during the early mob gatherings in front of our home. Back then they were only fined ten dollars and costs. In the words of James Newell, the Betterment Committee's leader, the committee had consistently talked against violence. Yet we were told that Howard Bentcliffe's fine was paid by a check on the funds of the Levittown Betterment Committee.

This latest arrest was what we had hoped would come. Bill and I, as well as our many sympathizers, had wrestled with the problem of getting law enforcement agencies to use their power to curb the characters responsible for the violence and intimidation. We were hoping the arrests would serve as a deterrent.

A few days later two more arrests were made. Again, Bentcliffe was one of them. He and Eldred Williams were arrested and charged with conspiracy for making and transporting a cross that had been burned on the lawn of our friend Peter Von Blum on September 22. Both were freed on $500 bail and scheduled for later hearings. Williams was the leader of the gang that loitered in the "clubhouse."

Thus—after two long months—peace finally came to Levittown and the Myerses. It was a pleasant and welcome peace, something we had not known since we left Bloomsdale Gardens. Gone were the outside agitators, the loiterers, the motorcades, the bugle blowing, the honking horns, the clapping hands, the loud auto radios. We could now notice the gorgeous roses blooming at the side of the garage, water the lawn, and admire the beauty of our new home.

The arrests came at a time when we were reaching the lowest ebb in our personal determination. We had tried desperately to maintain a spirit of love for our tormentors. In a way, we had succeeded. We had held out hope and faith that a ray of light would break through the clouds that had hovered over our home for the past two months. We had not necessarily expected our prayers to be answered in arrests, but they were, and it transformed the atmosphere of Levittown and gave us needed inspiration.

In our moments of weakness, we had talked of leaving. But what would that have accomplished? To withdraw was to admit defeat, and we held on with determination and courage to push back these defeatist thoughts. Perhaps the biggest factor in our personal determination was the many well-wishers who spared no detail to make our stay comfortable. Mail continually poured in. One letter came with two hundred fifty signatures. It was as if all two hundred fifty were giving us a pat on the back. At this point, we received little or no negative mail. We composed a general letter to send to all those who had written us:

> Dear Friend:
>
> Your letter has been a source of deep and lasting comfort to us, and we are grateful to the many hundreds who have shown their good will to our family.
>
> Although some have spoken loudly against us, literally hundreds from this and other parts of the world have shown that they too believe that all men are equal before God and that civil rights still exist in this country. To suffer for one's beliefs is better than to believe in nothing worth suffering for.

We would like to answer each message individually, but in order to acknowledge them reasonably soon this seemed the best way. We hope that others in similar circumstances may be sustained by the courage of your warmhearted gesture.

>With real thanks to each of you,
>Sincerely,
>William and Daisy Myers

This freedom from the "nerve war" that had been waged against us came none too soon. We saw less of the hostile faces and began to think that we might, after all, live in Levittown peacefully.

The next good news came when the telephone began ringing to tell us of a story in the afternoon papers. The Commonwealth of Pennsylvania, which had provided constant protection, was now taking further steps to bar any future acts of intimidation.

Chapter 11
Our Day in Court

Climaxing an intensive investigation by the Pennsylvania State Police, a petition for a permanent injunction was filed by the state Justice Department. The defendants named were eight Levittown residents who had key roles in the disturbances: Eldred Williams, James Newell, Howard Bentcliffe, Agnes Bentcliffe, John Bentley, David Heller, John Piechowski, and Mary Brabazon.

The temporary injunction was granted on October 23, 1957. A full hearing was set for December 9 in front of Judge Edwin Satterthwaite. Attorney General McBride said at the time, "I am confident that the vast majority of citizens of Levittown and Pennsylvania deplore the defendants' activities as inimical to the principles of a free and Democratic society and will join with us to foster better understanding in our communities."[33]

The complaint named each defendant and defined their intentions:

> To force the said Myers family to leave Levittown; to harass, annoy, intimidate, silence, and deprive of their rights to peaceful enjoyment of their property residents of Levittown who did not participate in the conspiracy or in any act designed to force the said Myers family to leave Levittown; to deprive the said Myers family and other residents of Levittown of their rights to personal security and equal protection of the laws; to interfere with and prevent law enforcement officers from performing their duties with the intent to deny the aforesaid residents of Levittown the equal protection of the laws.[34]

Then it listed the defendants' actions in detail, going far beyond just the mob demonstrations in front of our house. They had not only burned crosses at the Wechslers' and Peter Von Blum's houses, they also twice burned a cross at the home of John Preston. Mr. Preston had also received an envelope with the message, "Preston—You and Lafferty Beware! Keep your big Mouth Shut. The KKK Has Eyes. We Know your Every Move—Keep Your Mouth Shut."

Before the hearing for the permanent injunction opened, the lawyer for the Bentcliffes withdrew from the case. Eldred Williams was the only other defendant without an attorney. And David Heller was dropped from the suit because it was proved he did not participate.[35]

When I met the fanatical bigots face to face for the first time in the hallways of the courthouse, they appeared cowardly and retreating. To close my eyes momentarily, I could see them in previous days and nights as frightening monsters. As I looked at them now, they became trapped mice seeking the nearest hole in which to hide. The famous quotation by Sewell came to mind, "We shall be judged, not by what we might have been, but what we have been." They had seemed important people at the very beginning; now suddenly they appeared sober, drab, and quite subdued.

Newell tried to disassociate himself from his followers, but they boldly sought him out in the crowds. He tried to identify himself as an innocent bystander who

---

[33] "8 in Levittown Ordered to Stop Annoying Negro," *Evening Bulletin,* October 23, 1957, 5.
[34] *Commonwealth of Pennsylvania v. Williams et al.,* September 1957 term; "8 in Levittown Ordered to Stop Annoying Negro," *Evening Bulletin,* October 23, 1957, 5.
[35] "State Wants Court to Continue Ban as Peace Surety," undated newspaper clipping in author's files.

was just trying to do the most good for the most people. He would later say he only did "what the people wanted" him to do.

One of the defendants arrogantly approached Mr. McBride demanding to know if he would be paid for the day lost at work. Mr. McBride calmly asked to see the summons. After noting that the defendant was one of those charged with conspiracy to force us to leave, Mr. McBride answered, "If I were you, I'd be worrying whether or not I was going to jail."

I testified on the first day. Bill did not appear at the hearing since his testimony would likely have been identical to mine or at least repetitious on most of the facts. In all, forty-three people were called into court for the hearing, which lasted three days. In the middle of the week, a request by the defendants to have the charges dismissed was denied.[36]

As testimony wore on, we heard many stories, some very similar, others singularly frightening. The Klan connection we had suspected came to full light when Sgt. Adrian McCarr testified. When questioned by Mr. McBride, Sergeant McCarr said in addition to a letter from the Klan's imperial wizard, he found Klan applications in Howard Bentcliffe's possession. Sergeant McCarr also said that both Bentcliffe and Eldred Williams had both signed applications for membership in the Klan and that Williams had told him he wanted to join the Klan but "didn't have the $10 initiation fee."[37]

New information was uncovered during Sergeant McCarr's testimony. He said he had "found . . . an anonymous letter which had not been mailed to my knowledge to Wechsler relative to the cross burning at this home." The letter said:

> September 8, 1957
> Dear Mr. Wechsler:
> It is comforting I know to want to believe the cross burned on your lawn was a childish prank. But we know differently, don't we?
> It was purposely crudely constructed and was put there to let you know that, although the crowds have diminished, the feeling against you have not, nor will ever be.
> We are members of an organization that was born in the south. It is legal and it is chartered. Need I say more?
> We have some of the best legal talent in the country working behind the scenes for us making plans, which include yourself and the two Mr. M's.
> We've been working hard, we have positive proof of the part the NAACP played in the purchase of the home at 43 Deep Green—the names of the participants—how much each received for their part—everything we need to know. Believe me, Mr. W.; I would take off for parts unknown.
> Once we establish our facts in court, you can surely imagine the result. It will not only upset plans here; it will affect and destroy all such plans as was carried out in Dogwood for the nation. Inasmuch as these are not threats in this letter but facts—screening for fingerprints or handwriting is not necessary. A copy is being sent to (3) newspapers for publication.
> We are not an organization of terror as is commonly stated, but rather one with ideals which we believe are just and right. We are American

---

[36] Ibid.
[37] "Policeman Reveals Plan for Levittown Ku Klux Klan," December 10, 1957, newspaper clipping in author's files.

citizens, not "Commies" or "riff-raff" and we are fighting and will continue to fight for what we believe to be our constitutional right. We base our beliefs on the Bible which we interpret a bit differently than the so-called "Friends," the society there of who would like you to believe them Christians. I, the writer, come from ancestry of *true* Quakers, and believe me, we want no parts of such as they.

Think long—and think carefully—Mr. W.—pull out while you can.

We have the facts, believe me—and we are going to use them to our fullest advantage—when they are brought forth, it will upset all the plans of the NAACP, they will reach the heart of Washington, even to the Supreme Court.

Signed: A citizen born in the U.S.A.
Member of a legal charted organization.
R.E./The south[38]

Our neighbor testified about the impact the harassment had on his family:

> My two children are quite young ages, three and one. . . . They were awakened directly by the noise from outside the house. My wife was in a fairly distraught nervous state while most of these things were going on and, at one point, suggested that she and the children go to my mother's home in Trenton. . . . . My wife was afraid that perhaps there might be a mistake between my house and the Myers' home, as there are only those two homes on the corner. . . . I had a large group of people standing around on my lawn, and they dropped a number of cigarette butts and empty cigarette packages; there were a number of cans of beer, and things of that nature that I found strewn all over my lawn. The only solution that I found to the thing was my running my lawn sprinkler most of the night on the side of the house where the crowd would usually gather.

Our neighbor Peter Von Blum testified as well. "When I went out in the mob about 9:30 on the night of August 13, somebody threatened to beat me up. . . . I called Township Manager Henry Rolfe, Jr. and asked for police protection. He told me police were aware of the situation and didn't see any need to be at the scene."[39]

Reverend Harwick described how he was harassed by phone:

> I accepted the chairmanship of the Citizens' Committee very early on Saturday morning, the 17th, and we were then in the process of trying to organize a group within the community to work out a positive, peaceful, and Christian solution to the problem, and I believe my name appeared in print the first time on Saturday. The following night, Sunday night, we began receiving telephone calls. . . . I personally received about fifty or sixty. . . . The one type of call came from people who would not give their names; they used abusive language; they cursed; there were some veiled threats; there were some who said this is the KKK calling; there were others

---

[38] *Commonwealth of Pennsylvania v. Williams et al.,* September 1957 term.
[39] "State Wants Court to Continue Ban as Peace Surety."

who said this is a member of the white citizens council calling; and, on one occasion, they said, "How many children did you say you had, Reverend, is it three?" ... The other type of call came from people who were deeply disturbed by the thing that had happened. They were very much fearful for the loss of their property values, and so on, as it might develop in Levittown as a result of the Myers' moving, and they expressed a great deal of dislike, in some cases hatred, for me personally, because of the particular role I was playing in the community problem.[40]

Some of the defendants testified, too. John Bentley said that he enlisted members for the Levittown Betterment Committee and that 1,200 Levittown residents paid one dollar each to join.[41] He also said that when the committee first met, they voted on contacting the Ku Klux Klan, but the vote failed.

At the end of the hearing, Judge Satterthwaite told us to expect a long delay before a decision was handed down. In the meantime, on January 31, 1958, the trial for Howard Bentcliffe and Eldred Williams began. It ended in a mistrial that same day when Bentcliffe, who was acting as his own attorney, fainted in court. A week later, Williams admitted to building a cross which was then burned on a neighbor's property. At the end of February, Bentcliffe pled guilty to burning a cross and painting the KKK on the Wechslers' house. He was given a $250 fine and a year's probation.[42]

Much to our relief, on August 15, 1958, a year and two days after it all started, Judge Satterthwaite granted the permanent injunction, ruling that:

> The defendants and all other persons acting in concert or cooperation with them be, and they hereby are, enjoined from doing any of the following acts until further order of the Court: burning or causing to be burned fiery crosses, trespassing and affixing to the property of others or distributing on private property of others or littering the streets and public areas with inflammatory posters, scurrilous pictures, and leaflets and other printed matter, harassing or annoying the residents of Levittown by organizing, instigating or participating in motorcades, loud slamming of mail boxes, loud summoning of dogs by the appellation "nigger," setting off firecrackers, placing or causing to be placed in Levittown bombs or explosives of any kind whatsoever, in any manner threatening or intimidating any individual, or in any manner threatening the destruction of property, taking any acts of any kind whatever which seek by force, violence or intimidation to compel the removal or withdrawal of the said Myers from Levittown or by force, violence, or intimidation to prevent the sale of any property in Levittown to any Negro.[43]

We were finally assured a peaceful life in Levittown.

---

[40]*Commonwealth of Pennsylvania v. Williams et al.,* September 1957 term.
[41]"State Wants Court to Continue Ban as Peace Surety."
[42]"Defendant Faints, Mistrial Declared," February 1, 1958; "Cross Building Guilty in Bucks," February 7, 1958; and "Man Fined $250 in Cross Burning," February 26, 1958; all newspaper clippings in author's files.
[43]*Commonwealth of Pennsylvania v. Williams et al.,* September 1957 term.

Chapter 12
The Aftermath

Today—in 1960—the crisis of 1957 seems to be just a faded memory to the seventy thousand residents of Levittown. A stranger in Dogwood Hollow would see no evidence of the jeering crowds, police lines, vandalism, and violence that racked the neighborhood over two years ago. Some Levittowners describe the city as wonderful; others have told me they find the people here cold, indifferent, and unfriendly.

Once things settled down and the permanent injunction was in place, our lives changed. We became so involved with luncheons, dinners, overnight guests, and personal appearances that we had little time to feel sorry for ourselves or for retrospection. We counted nearly a month of dinner invitations received in Levittown alone. We were happy for these courtesies, particularly since some invitations were from residents in the higher-income Levittown neighborhoods. We found satisfaction in knowing that we could be accepted by Levittown's top social classes despite the hate peddlers of the Betterment group who felt that we were far below their economic and social level simply because our skin did not match theirs. Several parties were held in friends' homes as well as one in the local Congregational Church.

The international publicity surrounding Levittown brought some surprises. We met and corresponded with many famous people like Jackie Robinson and Martin Luther King Jr. We had the wonderful experience of spending a day as guests of Pearl Buck in her Bucks County home. She is such an unusual person; I'll never forget her.

Despite the many difficulties surrounding our move, we have never been lonesome since moving to Levittown. Too, we have always found much happiness as a family unit, and this made our lives easier at the time.

Some efforts were made in the community to bring the neighborhood together. The "Dogwood Hollow Neighbors" organized to "restore a friendly and harmonious atmosphere for all Dogwood Hollow residents." These people, who were mainly friendly toward us, met weekly at first, and then bimonthly, to discuss and plan a public meeting on the effect of integration on real estate values. This group did not enjoy one hundred percent success, but it did serve several purposes. Bill and I were able to meet the members personally and answer some of their questions and participate in their general discussions. Movies were shown, and people with experience in intergroup relations led discussions. A number of residents expressed interest in the group but found it impossible to attend meetings—or at least they gave some excuse. Some still feared reprisals from the Betterment Committee. One family said they liked Negroes but disliked Jews and would not attend. Eventually, the "Dogwood Hollow Neighbors" evolved into the Saturday Human Relations Workshop, which met at various Levittown schools, for a program consisting of speakers, movies, workshop groups, lunch, entertainment, and a panel discussion with an answer period.

Throughout our difficulties, a host of organizations worked in the background to support our right to live in Levittown. Among them were the National Council of Churches, Anti-Defamation League of B'nai B'rith, Philadelphia Fellowship Commission, AFL-CIO, Levittown Civic Association, Americans for Democratic Action, Women's International League for Peace and Freedom, YWCA,

Commission on Social Action of Reformed Judaism, American Friends Service Committee, Human Relations Council of Bucks County, National Association for the Advancement of Colored People, Veterans of Foreign Wars, Jewish War Veterans, Jewish Community Council, American Jewish Congress, and Levittown League of Women Voters. One can only speculate on the potential effect if some of the immobilized forces of the community had stood up to be counted on our side.

At the same time, the Levittown Ministers' Association could not agree on any united action and urged individual ministers to preach on tolerance. Some ministers heeded that call. The substitute minister of a local Presbyterian church came to our home and assured us his views were shared by the vacationing pastor. He told us he had made a fervent plea for understanding and tolerance in his church, promising to be of service when needed. His visit was inspiring, and I repeated to myself, "Of course, all people are not evil." Since that visit, we have not seen the permanent minister.

A local Lutheran minister said during his sermon, "A Christian may choose to move if he dislikes his next-door neighbor, and it is perfectly legitimate for him to be concerned about property values. But there is another area where the Bible speaks plainly: The Christian dare engage in no violence, no slandering, no threatening of law officers. 'Thou shalt love thy neighbor as thyself.' God let this happen to Levittown. To resist it any longer is to resist God. It can build spiritual power of the people. Here's a test of Christian mettle—to love a neighbor you don't think particularly desirable." This statement left me quite confused about the reverend's terminology of a Christian. I never knew that in the eyes of some people my God's children were undesirable.

Thankfully, the Reverend Dr. Fred Manthey of the Plymouth Congregational Church made us welcome and offered spiritual assistance. Our children attended their Sunday school, however, we attended church irregularly since our schedule was not yet normal. With the exception of Reverend Harwick, Reverend Manthey, Reverend Stevick, and Rabbi Fierverkey, no other Levittown ministers offered any assistance. Those ministers who did act on our behalf felt repercussions. A year after the Levittown incident, Reverend Manthey resigned from the Plymouth Congregational Church, saying that the National Board of Home Missions was forcing him out because he welcomed us to his church.[44]

Noticeably absent among the forces that worked on our behalf was the Catholic Church. In a conversation with a neighbor, I was told of strategy meetings held unnoticed in the basement of the local Catholic church. We've often wondered why a carload of men in clerical attire visited our neighborhood. They parked in front of our house and looked and talked. As they started to leave the car, newsmen and photographers swarmed on them. They were quite annoyed and left immediately without making known their reason for coming. Based on their clothes, we assumed that they were Catholic priests.

In the months after the injunction, Bill and I noticed little signs of both friendliness and bigotry still in our daily lives. As our pictures appeared in some newspaper or magazine, we were easily recognized. Strangers usually asked,

---

[44] "Pastor Who Aided Negroes Resigns: Minister in Levittown, Pa., Blames Church Pressure—Board Denies Charge," *New York Times*, Feb. 25, 1959.

"Pardon me, but are you the Myerses—the family that moved to Levittown?" Then they would express their shame at being white and congratulate us on pursuing our rights. The bigots who recognized us stared, rolled their eyes, or mumbled aloud at the supermarket, "So this is Daisy Myers . . . the troublemaker."

Some of what we experienced was totally unexpected. On Halloween we ran out of goodies three times and had to telephone friends to bring us a fresh supply. Later that night a knock came and three kids were at the door. One said, "My mommy has been waiting all night for your boys to come by for trick or treat, and since they didn't, we brought their candy over to them." I was overwhelmed by the experience. The mother introduced herself to Bill later at the food store and said, "We are your new neighbors. We are from New York."

A couple who lived next door to one of the most vicious of the "venom"-speaking women passed our home daily but didn't speak to us until two years and two weeks after the disturbances when the husband passed our house and waved, saying, "Hello, Mr. and Mrs. Myers."

Though harassment was banned by the court order, some undercurrents of hard feelings continued. No one who participated in the harassment was ever punished more than with a fine. Still, it was not surprising that the diehard racists found it difficult to accept the fact that law and order would prevail, and as long as it did, we would stay in Levittown.

Once when I was about to enter the grocery store, Howard Bentcliffe spat on the sidewalk as I passed.

Six months after our move, James Newell told a newspaper, "There are no legal means we can use to get them out. It's the law of the land. But I still feel Myers shouldn't be in Levittown."[45] Newell later ran for office as a committeeman for our precinct. He campaigned daily with a loudspeaker on his car driving throughout the neighborhood. In his southern drawl, he appealed for votes, saying, "You all know where I stand on the issues." When he would pass our house, he would say, "I only did what the people wanted me to do."

Indeed, the people showed that they knew where he stood. In the privacy of the polling booth, he was defeated three to one. We were gratified to see him rejected. It helped strengthen our original thoughts that the community was decent and did not condone the overt actions of the Betterment Committee. Equally important to note is that all of the other candidates who had been associated with the Betterment group also lost miserably.

Since Bloomsdale is in walking distance of Dogwood Hollow, Negro children from Bloomsdale had already integrated the school system, but there were no Negro teachers prior to 1957. The first Negro teachers were assigned shortly after we moved. As the news spread of Negroes teaching white children in the public schools, the Betterment group was riled again, but only to the extent of "whispered threats."

I found out how the experience had changed me when, accompanied by my friend Joan, I went to purchase a washing machine. I'd been shopping in this particular store for years. After the salesman had explained the various brands and I had made my decision, he began to make out the sales slip and asked my

---

"Levittown Now Settling Down to Normality Six Months after Ruckus over Racial Issue," *Trenton Sunday Times-Advertiser*, March 16, 1958.

name. He wrote, "Mrs. William . . .," then looked me over. He said, "Just a moment, please," and retreated to the back of the store.

"No washer here," I said to my friend.

She replied, "Gosh, how strange."

It seemed as if we waited an hour, but actually it was only minutes before he returned with three or four other dignified-looking gentlemen. I whispered to Joan, "Well, here it comes." Instead, he introduced himself as the head of the department and then introduced the other salesmen. They all shook my hand and said how much they admired my husband, and if I ever needed them to be sure to call. I thanked them and left, feeling embarrassed.

This incident illustrates one of the damaging effects those events had on us. We were already sensitive, and since moving to Levittown, I had allowed myself to become supersensitive, readily expecting the worst. That evening, recalling the day's events, I vowed to live as I now believe: the bigots are a small minority and the American people, for the most part, are kind and tolerant at heart.

My children were not sheltered from neighborhood attitudes either. Since they were too young for public school, we sent them to the nursery school at the William Penn Center to have some contact with other children. A few playmates would drop by now and then. Even a few of the children of Betterment members would come around, asking strange questions and noticing everything. Most of them could not understand why we were not "different," as their parents had probably told them. My children would watch them with questioning eyes.

After some months of the children playing together, the matter of race was introduced to my five-year-old son, William. He told me someone called him "black," and he could not understand why because his skin is brown.

Hearing the story, I felt the sudden heavy burden of trying to explain what the boy meant. Stalling for my own answer, I asked William what he had said when he was called black. "I told him he just didn't know his colors. I got a brown crayon and a black crayon and made a mark with each to show him the difference."

I wanted to know what happened next.

"He didn't say anything. He just stood there, looking first at the brown and then the black marks."

I was pleased with the child's handling of the matter and merely added that color does not make a difference in a person—we should think in terms of what kind of individual someone is rather than what color. I began to wonder how soon it would be before we would be compelled to give him a full explanation. How would we explain the Levittown situation and this complex business of race?

My three-year-old, Stephen, volunteered his race experience by saying, "Yeah, Mom, a boy called me 'black boy' down by the mailbox yesterday, and I called him 'green boy.'"

Other incidents were more ominous. Representatives of the Levittown Public Recreation Association visited us to ask if we would subscribe to a ticket to swim in the Levittown pools. We took the membership. When we decided to go for a dip, we were shocked at the conditions. There were no showers and the toilets were out of order. We could not help but wonder just how sanitary these public pools were and decided against returning. A few days later a neighbor called to advise against going to the Levittown pools, explaining that "they are laying in wait for you, and it would be awful for those kids of yours to be hurt." Finally, an official of the Recreation Association asked that we notify him before we planned to go swimming so that he could put the police on guard. I told him that would be unnecessary.

The experience in Levittown recalled earlier encounters with prejudice at swimming pools. In our area, at the end of every summer, white children were given swimming parties sponsored by the Recreation Association, but Negro children never had one because no pools in the area would admit them. When I worked in recreation, I had been told that if my group wanted to swim, it was my problem to find a pool. With no pools available to us, the Negro children had to settle for a wiener roast instead.

As it became clear that we were in Levittown to stay and the community would not go to pieces, the opposition hit a low in popularity, while the silent sympathizers emerged. We began to be told how horrified so many people were with what had happened. We realized that fear had gripped many who were afraid to openly express their convictions. Visitors would drop in from near and far to shake hands and offer words of encouragement. The news reports had been sensationalized to such an extent that a New York businesswoman felt it necessary to call Levittown before her visit to see if it was safe to come. Another woman called me from San Francisco to find out if "blood [was] running down Deepgreen Lane." She expressed her shame at fellow American whites and wished us good luck. A neighbor came by and stood in the doorway and cried for minutes. She then introduced herself, told me how sorry she was about the incident, and said, "I have wanted to come, to come badly, and now that I'm here, I don't know what to say. Just forgive them [the demonstrators]. I will come back when I am stronger."

Very few people realize how fear and terrorism can creep over a community. It started here with the toss of the first rock that broke our window. No one was hurt, so everyone was hesitant about acting to avoid any further violence. Though they may not have been afraid at first, their terror grew as the crowds became bolder. The Betterment leaders sought signers for their petition and threatened those who refused. During the solicitation of funds, one neighbor told them they were a "bunch of psychopaths."

As days and months passed, we gradually began to feel like the Myers family before August 13, 1957. We had time to ourselves and more time to enjoy our children. We kept up with the mail, which had dropped in volume, but there were always five or six letters a day. People all over the world were still interested to know what was happening to us. It took many weeks of work to handle the mail. Some letters we received are still waiting for a personal answer.

"Hello, Bill Myers," said a white acquaintance in a Levittown news store one day. "I don't know whether to congratulate you or call you a damn fool. I was at a poker game last night, and all the fellows were talking about the Myers situation and said you certainly have to respect a guy like you."

All we wanted to do was buy a house. We realized years ago, to our sorrow, that the housing market above all else stands as a symbol of racial inequality. No matter how renowned, wealthy, or prominent, the Negro cannot buy in a free and open market. How many times have we been tried and convicted on our right to purchase a home? How many thought us foolish to live where we were not wanted by the bigoted? How many thought we were right to pick a home of our own choosing? How many thought we were unwise to subject our children to this sort of thing?

It hurts a man's pride to see something he wants, something he has the money for, and be told he can't buy it because he is a certain color or of a particular religion. It hurts him to watch his children suffer—suffer dearly—for the evils of segregation and discrimination. When buying a house, children are any parent's first consideration. Negro citizens and other minorities are just as interested in opening doors to better educational and economic opportunities as any other human beings. Does the home have ample and safe playing space, good schools, adequate recreational facilities? Those were—and still are—our concerns.

A house is more than protection from the weather. It indicates social status and reflects aspirations and ideals. A house reflects personality. Most often one is identified with his surroundings and associates. What a tragedy that many people of minority races are falsely identified because they are *forced* to stay within the walls of the "black belt." A local teacher said to me, "I have the nicest, most refined little colored boy in my class. He is the most perfect child I've had in years, and can you imagine he came from the Terrace [a segregated, low-rent, over-crowded housing project in this area]?" Why was the teacher surprised? Because he lived in the Terrace. We all tend to prejudge individuals by their habitat. We label people by thinking their surroundings are who they are.

The overemphasis on "Negro crime," "Negro illegitimacy," "Negro cultural lag," and the other clichés reflects ignorance of the facts. People who use those words do not know what Dr. Charles Drew did to make possible the blood plasma program or the scientific contributions of Dr. George Washington Carver. Negroes have given to America some of the richest folk culture—spirituals, work songs, blues, jazz, and folklore. Negroes are novelists, biographers, poets, and social scientists. They are active in civic, state, and national and international affairs. There are Negro scientists, newsmen, research specialists, physicians, lawyers, teachers, and so on.

It is just as silly to say that Negroes are "inferior" as it is to say whites are "superior." All races have their good and bad. We have slums, crime, and illegitimacy—so does everyone else. Most of our poor, rundown environment is inherited secondhand from the white man who is free to move on to a new and inviting area of better living. More liberty for minorities does not mean less freedom for others but would bring greater freedom for all. White people who have contact with people of other races learn to respect individuals for their worth and are not concerned with "tolerating" differences.

How distasteful it is to read about certain southern office-seekers who have no more than a third-grade education and run on a platform of "white supremacy." Some of the key leaders in the Betterment Committee were no better qualified and could lay no claim to being responsible citizens. Yet they felt they could accept the roles of leadership in spewing hatred over Levittown, because the only "sin" we committed was being black.

Negroes recognize these years as an opportunity to wipe out the racial injustices of a hundred years. They accept the challenge, but they want other Americans to realize that individual merit and accomplishment must be the lone yardstick for measuring all human beings. There will be sit-down strikes, passive objections, and continual unrest until Negroes are given complete freedom and treated as first-class citizens.

Much of the Negro society's deviant behavior is due to social isolation, economic deprivation, emotional frustration, and the lack of cultural outlets. However, the younger Negro is different, and I pray for more each day. Already the number is large, but no public emphasis is put on those who pay taxes, buy homes, save money, live clean lives, and are active in church and other community institutions. Too much is heard of the knife-wielders, muggers, gamblers, dope pushers. The Negro is like any other American—as responsible as his environment permits him to be.

The presence of a minority person in a white neighborhood as a servant, trash collector, caretaker, or janitor hardly ever attracts unfavorable criticism from whites. Yet when nonwhites come to live under circumstances that imply equal status, some whites react with hate and fear. Just as one Negro is not the social equal of another, we cannot say that one white man is the social equal of another white man. Truck drivers and doctors are on different social levels regardless of skin color, but a white doctor and a Negro doctor would certainly have something in common to talk about.

Some Levittowners are ashamed of their lowly beginnings in Philadelphia and upstate Pennsylvania, and for the first time, they own something they cherish. As they struggle, some are just clinging by their fingernails to achieve equal status with their neighbors. Social position is important to these people. Many of them felt threatened when we moved in. Who would they look down on now? Those who are socially secure seem unconcerned for they know where they stand, while the insecure feel threatened to share their neighborhoods and preach loudest against social equity among whites and Negroes.

As Bill and I reflected on the neighbors' fears of loss of "status," we realized that other reasons may have motivated them, too. One could speculate on the origins—perhaps an unhappy childhood, a job failure, or unsatisfactory relationships with members of their social group. These people were compelled to hate, and we were a convenient target.

It was with a touch of sadness that I read of the suicide of one of our neighbors who was a principal agitator in the crisis. He was quoted by a national magazine during the height of the crisis as saying, "A lot of people moved to Levittown to get away from colored people." His suicide indicated there was a lot more than colored people that he felt the need to escape from. Indeed, he ran from life itself.

After we moved to Levittown, a neighbor whose husband was a bus driver said, "Oh, I don't mind too much if a Negro like Ralph Bunche wanted to move next to me."[46] There is no choosing of neighbors on the open market. You seek a house, and factors like schools, stores, shopping areas get priority. If there were opportunities to select neighbors, I'm afraid some of the folks who harassed us would not be included by many citizens, including the Myerses. Rejecting

---

[46]*Editor's note:* Ralphe Bunche (1904-71) was a civil rights activist who acted as mediator for the United Nations in Palestine in the late 1940s and won the Nobel Peace Prize in 1950. See: http://www.nobel.se/peace/laureates/1950/bunche-bio.html.

neighbors because they do not own a shiny automobile or new furniture sounds silly, and it is. It is the same logic as choosing a neighbor based on skin color. I suppose that neighbor never considered whether Ralph Bunche would want to live next to her.

A recent survey in our neighborhood indicated that many residents didn't mind a Negro moving next to them "if they are like the Myerses." It seems the qualifications have changed considerably from Ralph Bunche to William Myers.

The Betterment group voiced two principal objections to us remaining in Levittown: 1) Negroes would bring property values down and (2) intermarriage would become possible.

Without the benefit of equal-status contact, and based on inherent prejudices and obeisance to the stereotype, the bigoted want to perpetuate the belief that not only are Negroes inferior, but that they live and act that way, too. As a result, when a nonwhite moves into a neighborhood, the first reaction is to run, run, run without stopping to think. I was surprised when a neighbor with whom we had socialized on several occasions said, "The Myerses might be a nice family, but what about the others to follow?"

Another neighbor said, "The Myerses look like a nice family, but every time I look at him, I can see two thousand dollars off my house." This belief can be an excellent rationalization for prejudice.

Depreciation of property values after nonwhites move into a previously all-white neighborhood can be attributed to a number of reasons. In most cases, Negroes are blamed for situations they have inherited from whites—homes in older neighborhoods where deterioration has already begun. In other cases, the price of the house is so high that upkeep and living expenses become a burden to the new owner, and it becomes necessary to take in roomers or share parts of the house to help meet mortgage payments.

Whites also play a role in determining property values. If white residents hurriedly move out when a Negro moves to a neighborhood or so-called restricted area, the market becomes overrun and an oversupply of houses will be up for sale in a short period. Values drop because homeowners cannot sell. Sometimes pressure is put on other residents to sell when a nonwhite family moves in and others of the same race are eager to get into the same area. Four other Negro families have moved into Levittown since we came and the price range has remained stable.

The fear of intermarriage is often injected into discussions of interracial housing and race relations by the prejudiced. A Levittown mother who had been friendly called me one day excitedly. "Oh, Mrs. Myers, I had to call and tell you that a Negro man made a pass at my daughter on the bus, and I want you to do something. This sort of thing just can't happen after your move-in and everything." I held the receiver almost limp as this well-intentioned mother made her plea.

No one is compelled to marry outside of his race. One has to stop and ponder if such fear-possessed persons are sincere. I can only say that a person usually marries someone who looks much like they do, someone who has similar background and interests. However, there are cases where people of different backgrounds do marry. For example, last year Stephen Rockefeller of the wealthy Rockefeller family married Anne Marie Rasmussen, who had been a maid for his family. Her minister said at the wedding, "Your example shows that real love, which is from God, breaks down all social and conventional barriers. That love is in accordance with the love of God. The love of God is universal. He loves everybody, and in His eyes we are equals."

Successful interracial marriages are not limited to only black and white. They could also be Japanese-American or Chinese-American. They occur because the persons involved are intelligent and mature. For some individuals, the question of intermarriage is no more serious than marriages of interfaith or a poor white man marrying a rich white Christian woman. If the parties are truly in love, then everything else seems secondary. Intermarriage will occur—and has since the remotest times—whether there is segregation or integration.

False reports and rumors occasionally still fly through Levittown, but this is typical of all small cities. Since we moved in, there has been no mass exodus of whites, nor have property values dropped as some people feared. However, those who cannot sell their homes hurriedly during these days of recession and unemployment are quick to blame the Myerses. Some homes have been sold, some rented, but this is a normal turnover for a community of this kind.

A frequent question asked is, "Have the people of Levittown accepted you yet?" It is an irritating query. We wonder why we're never asked if Levittown measures up to our expectations. We have no apologies for being Negroes, nor are we in the habit of defending our actions for having selected Levittown as our home. Blindness and prejudicial thinking prevent some people from understanding that some Negroes surpass some white people in social and economic achievement. Toleration connotes inferiority and implies some undesirable quality. There is condescension in the word acceptance.

I was driving to Trenton one day when I noticed an elderly lady waiting for the bus. I offered her a ride, and she accepted gratefully, stating she had been waiting quite a while. We chatted about the weather, the traffic, and last, Levittown. She introduced herself, finally, and said she had been visiting her daughter here and now was on her way to Newark to visit her son before her return to England. I had noticed the English accent and was enjoying it.

She asked, "What is your name?" I told her and she replied, "Why, your name is so familiar to me, I can't imagine."

I thought to myself, could she be one of many who wrote us from England? We received a number of letters from various places in England. I told her who I was and she seemed stunned. She reached over, patted me on the shoulder and said, "When I read about the trouble in the news, I said an old proverb my mother used to say to me—'Sticks 'n stones will break your bones, but words will never harm you.' I am happy and delighted to be able to say them to you, face to face." She continued, "And may God bless you and your family."

I dropped her off at the train station thinking just how *far-reaching* this Levittown crisis had been. Some letters we received from overseas said that their people watched closely the treatment of minorities here. Many believed there could be no international amity unless America first sought peaceful relations with her own colored people, and then other colored people of the free world.

Chapter 13
Life after Levittown

It's been over forty years since I wrote the other chapters of this book. Much has happened to the Myers family since then.

Life for Bill and me and the children eventually returned to normal. Much to our relief, most of the time we were just another family, out of the public eye. Our family was complete with the birth of our last child and youngest son, Barry, in November 1959.

We stayed in our pink rancher in Levittown for five years. In 1962, Bill got a job as superintendent of the state finance building in Harrisburg, and we moved back to central Pennsylvania. This time we had no problem finding a home. I'll never forget that house, it was so beautiful and unusual. The single-family home stood on Fifteenth Street in Harrisburg, an integrated neighborhood. The house had parquet floors, mahogany wood, wide windowsills, a third floor, a basement, an attic, and a wraparound porch. I loved that house.

I commuted to York to teach sixth grade at Lincoln Elementary School. Bill later got a job at York Shipley as a refrigeration/air conditioning engineer. He was badly needed because they were a heating company and didn't have people who knew air conditioning.

So we moved again, this time back to York. While we were shopping for our next home, real estate agents took us through many neighborhoods. I remember one agent, who was Jewish, asking us about our Levittown experience. We said to him, "How would you like it if you had plenty of money and couldn't buy the house you wanted?"

We looked at East York and West York, among other places, before deciding on the Arlington Park development in the Dallastown School District. When we bought our home, very few of the houses standing today had been built. The area was mostly wooded. The neighborhood was friendly, and we were welcomed with plenty of goodies. Neighbors brought their children to meet ours. Bill installed a basketball net so our home was the house where other kids came—all kinds of kids played in our yard.

All four Myers children graduated from Dallastown Area High School. William attended West Chester State College (now University), where he majored in education and went on to teach school. He now owns his own courier service in the Philadelphia area. Stephen is in law enforcement in Boston. They have very few memories of what happened in Levittown. In high school, Lynda was in the Honor Society and went to Austria in a student exchange program. I remember some opposition from people who said they couldn't send Lynda because Austrians wouldn't be comfortable with a black person. I told them, "Well, if you don't send her, you'll hear from me." She made the trip and was treated very well. After graduation, Lynda went to Penn State University and now teaches at the Yorktowne Business Institute. Her son, James, attends Millersville University. Barry moved the longest distance from home; he is a construction engineer living in Las Vegas.

I went into guidance counseling in elementary school and then into administration. By the time I retired from the York City school system in 1979, I was principal of Ferguson Elementary. I was bored, so retirement didn't last long. Bill was working part-time at the Yorktowne Hotel, where he became acquainted with

U.S. Representative William Goodling. He mentioned my boredom, and Mr. Goodling told him to have me come in and talk to him. I became a congressional assistant and held the job for almost twenty years before retiring in 1999. This time I stayed retired.

My husband, Bill, retired from Shipley in 1986 and died of lung cancer in 1987. He was my best friend, and I miss him every day.

When I think back over all of this—what happened in Levittown—I wonder how we made it through those days. The hardest part was going to sleep at night. It seems so stupid now. When we lived in that area, there was Bloomsdale Gardens and Levittown. Now Bloomsdale Gardens is part of Levittown. It's like we moved from Levittown to Levittown.

But as I said in the beginning of this book, what happened to me and to my family prepared us for who we are now—stronger human beings. The Myers family has not only survived but thrived while seeking a part of the American dream: to have a comfortable home. No one should ever be punished for that.

Epilogue

It is hard to believe that 10 years have gone by since my mother, Daisy Myers, passed in 2011. A lot has happened during that time. Civil and political unrest have been paramount, resulting in the Me-Too movement, the Time's Up movement, the Black Lives Matter movement, the Capitol Hill insurrection, the Occupy Wall Street protest, the Unite the Right rally in Charlottesville that led to the death of Heather Heyer, the Stop Asian Hate movement, and a number of other events. Particularly after several Black people were killed by police under questionable circumstances, protests and upheaval were triggered in many cities throughout the nation; for example, Ferguson (the shooting death of Michael Brown), Baltimore (Freddie Gray's death while in police custody), New York City (Eric Garner's death after being placed in a chokehold, Louisville (Breonna Taylor mistakenly shot to death), and Minneapolis (the George Floyd murder) to name a few. Predominantly peaceful demonstrations and some violent protests erupted throughout America and the world.

I often wonder how my parents would react to these acts of discord and turmoil that resulted from such prejudice and hate. How would they compare these situations to the events that surrounded the Civil Rights movement and the Levittown Crisis? Would they support the movements and protests? What advice could they share with the country? It would be truly fascinating to hear their perspectives on the current climate of our nation. I believe they would be honest and supportive of the steps the nation is taking to address hundreds of years of injustice and inequality.

I often marvel at how my parents handled their experiences stemming from prejudice and hate and stayed focused to gain their dreams and stand up for their rights. My parents did not speak often about the Levittown Crisis. It was not something they would boast about. They viewed the experience as a time when they had to do what they had to do so that our family could live the "American Dream." I still find it amazing how my mother was so forgiving after facing such animosity and maliciousness. How she endured the cross burnings, racial slurs, instances of denied service, and death threats is beyond believable to me. In 1999, when the previous Bristol Township mayor Sam Fenton invited my mother back to Levittown to publicly apologize for the events of 1957, my mother graciously accepted the request for forgiveness. She enjoyed her time back in Levittown! To be honest, after facing such frightful encounters as my parents did, I am not sure I would have been as gracious to accept Levittown's apology. To even go back to Levittown at all might have been very difficult for me.

My mother was quite special in how she did not rest in hate. She would do anything to secure the dreams and wishes she had for her family. She did not start this journey to become famous or celebrated. She simply wanted a nice home for her growing family. That is probably the reason she was dubbed the "Rosa Parks of the North." Ms. Parks simply wanted a seat on the bus to rest her weary body. She was not looking to start a major social movement, just as my mother was not trying to throw more logs on the fire for the Civil Rights movement. My mother just wanted a home.

My mother, Daisy Myers, was undeniably a strong, courageous, and compassionate woman who believed she was entitled to all the rights and privileges afforded to white Americans. She had no hate in her heart, even after facing such horrible circumstances. To put it like my mother would say, "We love too seldom and hate too often." We can all take a lesson from her book and be more compassionate, empathetic, understanding, tolerant, and accepting. She often said that life was like a beautiful garden of flowers. There are so many different colors, shapes, and varieties peacefully growing together.

Lynda P. Myers, 2021